Risk Perception, Awareness and Prevention Measures to Reduce Underage Drinking and the Illegal Purchase of Alcohol in Malta

Duncan Aaron Borg Ellul

DISSERTATION.COM

Boca Raton

Risk Perception, Awareness and Prevention Measures to Reduce Underage Drinking and the Illegal Purchase of Alcohol in Malta

Dissertation.com
Boca Raton, Florida
USA • 2008

ISBN-10: 1-59942-672-2
ISBN-13: 978-1-59942-672-3

RISK PERCEPTION, AWARENESS
AND PREVENTION MEASURES
TO REDUCE UNDERAGE DRINKING AND
THE ILLEGAL PURCHASE OF ALCOHOL IN MALTA

by

DUNCAN AARON BORG ELLUL

Reference no: 12199

A dissertation submitted in partial fulfillment of
the requirements for the degree of

M.Sc. in Security and Risk Management

Supervisor: Ms Tracey Dodman

Department of Criminology

University of Leicester

The Friars, 154 Upper New Walk

Leicester, LE1 7QA

United Kingdom

DEDICATION

To my fiancée Marie Claire. I could never have done this without you.

Thanks for your understanding, patience and support and for your never-ending love.

ACKNOWLEDGEMENTS

A project such as this would be incomplete without thanking

all those who helped me make it possible.

Studies of this nature would have been impossible without the continuous support and patience of Ms. Tracey Dodman, my thesis supervisor. I would like to express my deepest gratitude for her dynamic guidance and help through this process and for keeping me focussed in my research. Her thoughtful queries, observations and comments have worked as triggers to some key insights and analyses.

Special thanks to...

...Rita Jo and Emidio, for being after my parents during these last five years and for their great help and continuous support. Our conversations and work together have greatly influenced this thesis.

...My brother Kurt and his fiancée Anneliese, my father Martin and my grandfather Freddie for their encouragement during the course of study.

Special memories go to my mother Stella who passed away on 14th December 2000.

Chai, who gave enthusiastic moments in the better of his days.

My final thanks go to all those who took interest in my project and supported it including the staff at the Department of Criminology, University of Leicester, United Kingdom.

No effort goes in vain and none has.

ABSTRACT

This dissertation examines the social context of underage drinking in terms of crime, mental disorder and social disability. The perception of risk and awareness of Maltese young people plays a significant role in the study. Through this study, it was found out that underage drinking in Malta is a problem and that students have misconception about Laws on alcohol. It was also established that the Law in Malta is neither being supported by the community nor strictly enforced.

The study has reviewed the literature, which documented the importance, nature and extent of underage alcohol use in Malta. During the course of study, it was determined that young people are subjected to excessive pressure from school, parents, peers and/or other social reasons.

The literature review has shown that if a person abuses alcohol, he or she might become an alcoholic. Whilst drinking may be seen as normative and socialised behaviour, binge drinking in young people is linked to risk-taking, sex, fights, accidental injuries, suicide, deaths and crime. The literature also revealed that the younger a person begins to drink, the greater the chance he or she will develop a problem with alcohol later in life.

Based on the study being conducted, suggestions and recommendations are proposed on the wide range of strategies - from stricter enforcement of the Laws, relating to the sale of alcohol to minors; to prevention, treatment, rehabilitation and after-care.

Duncan Aaron Borg Ellul

TABLE OF CONTENTS

APPENDICES

LIST OF FIGURES

LIST OF TABLES

PHOTOGRAPHS

An Introduction

1.1 Introduction

Maltese people are worried about young people taking drugs and many parents are afraid that their children might fall into this risk. As the drug problem in Malta is being addressed, the alcohol problem, which can just do the same damage to one's health is being somewhat ignored. Young people can obtain alcohol in many different ways, as alcohol is legally and ready available for everyone in Malta. They can get it from friends or parents, a selling store, at home, in supermarkets, pubs, clubs, discos, restaurants and at village feasts. In Maltese term, village feasts are known as *festi tar-raħal*.

Bars are the most frequented venues for young people to drink. Hiring a flat in Malta's Mecca of entertainment, Paceville is an apt setting for drinking activities of young males and females. Flats are available to young people who cannot participate in the drinking activities taking place in bars and clubs.

The prospect of young people's parents drinking alcohol are also creating confusion in our children minds, as it is very difficult for our young people to understand why alcohol is dangerous. In this country, underage drinking uncovers serious implications, for the health of youngsters, juvenile justice, criminal justice and education systems.

1.2 Aims and Objectives of the study

Maltese researchers like Bezzina et al., 1997 and Muscat, et al., 2002 have indicated in their studies that underage drinking is a problem and that children in Malta are exposed to alcohol quite early in their lives. This is mainly discussed in Chapters 2 and 4. It appears from the surveys of Bezzina, et al., 1997 and Muscat, et al., 2002, that young people have low level of awareness, as they are increasing in the level of alcohol consumption. The researcher has attempted to gather as much of information with regard to Maltese Literature and Statistics regarding underage purchase, possession and consumption of alcohol and cases of persons in possession of false ID cards. It seems however, that in Malta, such data is limited or not available (Appendix C).

This research study examines the problem of underage alcohol use in Malta. It focuses on attitudes and experiences of alcohol among 13-15 year olds and on the prevention strategies aimed to reduce this problem. The researcher aims to provide knowledge through prevention and intervention strategies directed at the individual, family, school and the community, to reinforce the message that underage drinking is dangerous. As Gill (1996:16) states, we need '…to educate people about the dangers and put them on guard'.

1.3   Rationale for choice of topic

The rationale for the choice of this topic was to explore the experience of alcohol in the context of young people's lifestyle (13-15 years old). The researcher plans to assess the impact of alcohol use on young people's productivity and their social behaviour. The perception of risk and awareness of Maltese young people will play a significant role in the study. The issues discussed in this dissertation do relate to the course materials provided by the Department of Criminology, University of Leicester, especially on Social Crime Prevention. Such methods however, will be adapted according to the research being studied.

1.4   Hypotheses

Underage drinking in Malta is a problem for various reasons.

- Young people are subjected to excessive pressure from school, parents, peers and/or other social reasons to an extent that they misuse alcohol and put their health and of others at risk.

- The Law however is being neither supported by the community nor strictly enforced, particularly at venues of entertainment. Young people resort to drinking and retailers ascertain themselves by flaunting the Law.

1.5   Research questions

To test the researcher's hypotheses, the study therefore sets out to answer the following research questions.

- What is the attitude of young people aged 13-15 towards alcohol drinking?
- From where do young people consume alcoholic beverages most?
- What are the prevention methods used to reduce under age drinking in Malta particularly at venues of entertainment?

Recommendations from this study will be discussed in Chapter 5, for the perusal of the Maltese Government, National and Local Non-Profit Agencies, Professional Associations and for the Public - to increase the low level of awareness with regards to the misuse and abuse of alcohol drinking in Malta.

1.6 Methodology

This section deals with the methods used to investigate the answers to the research questions. A survey in Malta was conducted in State and Non-State schools of boys and girls aged 13-15. The research tools used were the written questionnaire and focus group discussions. The researcher assured the Confidentiality and Anonymity of all participants and was given in writing in the questionnaire. Observational methods were also used in this study, to observe young people's drinking lifestyles at the centre of entertainment – Paceville and at the village *festi*. In the observation methodology, the researcher mainly focused on Paceville and the events of young people in Paceville reported during the Christmas Season.

1.7 Sources of information used for Literature Review

The method used in this research will include a detailed Literature Review conducting using several sources of information such as the University of Malta library, course materials, books and journals. A computerised literature search was also conducted on the Internet. For data collection and data analysis, Microsoft Excel was used, operating in a Windows environment.

1.8 Ethical considerations

Covering letters from Ms. Tracey Dodman, Course Director at the Department of Criminology, University of Leicester were obtained (Appendix A, copy of a sample letter). Permission for conducting research in State schools in Malta was given by Mr. Joseph Magro, Director, Planning & Development at the Education Division and by Dr. Joseph F. Grima, Assistant Director for conducting research in Non-State schools. These approvals were obtained prior the commencement of the research study (Appendix B).

1.9   Course of study

This study is composed of the following:

- An introductory chapter (chapter 1), including a description of the issues being investigated and background information regarding the area of study.
- Chapter 2 - literature review.
- Chapter 3 - the methodology section.
- Chapter 4 - presentation and discussion of the results for the data collected.
- Chapter 5 - the conclusions and recommendations to the study and a set of guidelines.

Literature Review of Related Literature and Research

2.1 Introduction

The literature review in this chapter is devoted to recent empirical research concerning underage drinking and the illegal sale of alcoholic beverages to minors. Alcohol effects on frequent alcohol users with regards behaviour, social adjustment and interpersonal relations, will also be discussed in the study. Problems associated with this phenomenon will also be explored, such as the health risks and the impact of alcohol use on the individual's productivity and criminal offence.

2.2 What is alcohol?

Alcohol is a colourless, volatile, and pungent liquid, having the chemical formula C_2H_5OH. It is presented in fermented beverages such as beer, wine, champagne, and liquors. Arabian alchemists, who named it Al Kohl (Rockerbie, 1999), first discovered the production of alcohol by distillation.

One standard drink of beer (285 ml) or one standard drink of wine (100 ml) contains 10 g of alcohol and approximately 300 kilojoules (70 calories) each depending on the type of drink. New drinks on the market such as alcoholic colas, soda water and lemonade have similar alcohol content to beers and ciders, table wines, fortified wines, liqueurs and distilled drinks (Public Health Service, 1996). Alcohol strengths are easy to understand when expressed as a percentage by volume. Typically advantages are: Ciders (1-8%), beers (3½-10%), 'natural' wines (8-14%), vermouths and aperitif wines (18%), dessert, sweet and postprandial wines (Sherry, Port, Muscatel) (18-22%), cordials made of flavoured spirits (Anisette, Curacao, Maraschino (25-40%), spirits (40-70%) (Hickman, 2003a: 30).

Legal systems have refrained from laying down a Blood Alcohol Count rate (BAC) because an amount of alcohol can affect people differently. Members of the Medical Professions propose rough indications as to how particular BAC rates are likely to affect the normal (Appendix D) human being (Knight, 1997:178).

2.2.1 Alcohol and associated risks

Mason, (1983:263) argues that 'Alcohol is a critical depressant. It is the higher and most recently evolved brain functions that are first affected by depressants. The immediate effect of dose of alcohol is to inhibit those cerebral functions that are associated with orderly community behaviour and with fine critical judgments; an illusion of cerebral stimulation is thus precipitated'.

One needs to take into consideration the possible severity of alcohol and understand the risks associated with alcohol drinking. Alcohol related problems namely health-related issues, economic issues and crime problems affect all segments of society (U.S. Department of Health and Human Services, 1992), including family and friends.

If alcohol is taken in large quantities or mixed with drugs, it can be harmful to the human body. Symptoms of alcohol poisoning may include vomiting, loss of consciousness, cold and clammy skin and slow or irregular breathing. Drinking excessive alcohol can also make a person dehydrated (a term used to describe the loss of water from the body). Heavy drinking may affect adults as well as young people in terms of violence, disorder, and accidents. 'There may be symptoms of withdrawal for example such as hangovers, occurring when there is an abrupt fall in the alcohol level and a growing absorption in activities, which involve drinking, such as drinking at home and at leisure places' (Lintner, 1991:62).

In a publication by the British Medical Association, the long-term effects and risks of alcohol consumption are described as follows:

'Heavy drinkers risk developing liver diseases, for example, alcoholic hepatitis, liver cancer, cirrhosis, or fatty liver (excess fat deposits that may lead to cirrhosis). High blood pressure and strokes may also result from heavy drinking. Inflammation of the stomach (gastritis) and peptic ulcers are most common in alcoholics (Henry, 1998:441), who also have a higher than average risk of developing dementia (irreversible mental deterioration)'.

Drinking too much alcohol can cause drunkenness. Drunkenness or binge drinking appear later and usually there is a period of two years between the first consumption of alcohol and the first episode of drunkenness (Single and Leino, 1998). Drunkenness can also lead to unplanned and unsafe sex. In April 2002, all-women colleges in the US reported a 150 percent increase in drink-related sexual activity leading to steep rise in sexually transmitted disease (Hickman, 2003b: 158).

Drinking in moderation however, is neither undesirable nor dangerous. It may actually be associated with better health and greater longevity; but, where should one draw the line? The recommended daily amounts for women drinking alcohol are 2-3 units whilst for men 3-4 units a day are enough. According to the Department of Health (DOH), this is considered to be safe drinking (DOH, 1995).

2.2.2 *Alcohol, pleasure, and sociability*

According to the Home Office, (2004), 'the drinking of alcohol is widely accepted and associated with socializing, relaxing, and pleasure'. Some fear that endorsing any consumption of alcohol might lead to abuse. Violence, injury to others, fights with the police and sexual abuse may all be consequences of heavy alcohol drinking. Pleasure and sociability are an integral part of the occasional consumption of alcohol and in most cultures, drinking is an integral part of celebration. Particular sub-cultures create their own values (Scarman, 2001a (1): 4-16).

Whilst drinking may be accepted as a normative or a socialising behaviour, intoxication in young people is linked to crime. Associations between alcohol use, criminal activity and antisocial behaviour have been established in few British studies (Newcombe, et al., 1995; Deehan, 1999) and it was discovered that regular young drinkers are much more likely to have a criminal record than those who do not drink or only drink occasionally. The relationship between alcohol use and criminal or antisocial behaviour is illustrated in the Fergusson, Lynskey and Horwood Study (1996a) demonstrating that young people who misused alcohol had significantly higher rates of both violent and property offences.

2.3 Alcohol abuse and misuse

According to the World Book Dictionary (Barnhart, et al., 1992a: 10), abuse means 'to use wrongly; make bad use of; misuse' whilst the word misuse is 'to use for the wrong purpose; use improperly' (Barnhart, et al., 1992b: 1331). Alcohol abuse is defined by the World Book Medical Encyclopaedia (1995: 22) as 'the improper use of alcohol, a misapplication that can lead to alcoholism. Alcoholism involves a powerful "craving" or uncontrollable need for alcohol. This craving overrides the ability to stop drinking. Symptoms of alcohol dependence include craving for a drink of alcohol, inability to stop or limit drinking of alcohol and needing greater amounts of alcohol to feel the same effect' (The World Book Medical Encyclopaedia, 1995: 22).

An alcohol abuser is one who drinks beyond sobriety or who mixes alcohol with other chemical substances, but who does not yet have a chemical dependency on alcohol (The World Book Medical Encyclopaedia, 1995: 22). The consumption of alcohol is a normative experience among young people with considerable potential for abuse. Alcohol misuse is a risk factor, which gives rise to physical, psychological and social harm and is associated with anti-social behavior and public disorder. Studies report that young people's drinking experience starts either during the pre-adolescent or adolescent period is associated with an increased likelihood of developing alcohol abuse or dependence later in life (NIAAA, 2003a).

2.3.1 *Alcohol misuse and stress*

Stress is strongly associated with alcohol misuse as a self-medication 'therapy' for life stressors (Stress Management, 2004). Problem drinkers are characterised by having numerous personal and family problems. Indeed, individuals with a family history of alcohol show greater alcohol-induced stress dampening (NIAAA, 2003b). The results of several studies have shown that children from alcoholic families report higher levels of depression and anxiety and exhibit more symptoms of generalized stress (i.e., low self-esteem) than do children from non-alcoholic families (Anderson, et al., 1983: (3) 174-187).

Another important stress factor associated with young people is the examinations period. In Malta, students undergo one of the most stressful periods of their lives - the 'GCSE' level examinations. With institutes, university places and potential careers to be decided, students often find that the few weeks of examination time are the most pressurising on their young lives. Some students might resort to drink alcohol to relax when their study day is over, or after they have completed an exam. Alcohol drinking may lead to irritability, which will increase stress and thus reduce the short-term memory.

2.3.2 *Alcohol abuse and binge drinking*

A number of terms are used to describe these states; chronic drinking, alcohol misuse, heavy drinking, binge drinking, regular drinking and hazardous drinking. Binge drinking is defined as having five or more drinks in a row (Primedia Company, 2004). The current plethora of terms used does not advance our understanding of alcohol use and consumption across the population in general, or among adolescents or young people in particular. Wechsler (1995: 982-985) found a link between binge drinking (5/4 or more drinks in a row) and students who experienced problems such as committing vandalism and being involved with the police as well as personal injury.

The extent of the phenomenon of binge drinking can vary considerably from region to region. Studies indicate that in the United Kingdom, less than one in ten 13 year olds have not tried alcohol and half of those aged 13 to 16 binge. The young in Britain, including young women, are the biggest young drinkers in Europe and Spain. Italy and Greece complain that the British have through exported football and hooliganism to Europe. This is often the result of binge drinking (Hickman, 2003c: 183).

Adolescents with friends who drink are more likely to drink as well and the influence of peers on adolescent alcohol consumption is predictive of binge drinking. Peer group pressure, parental alcoholism, divorce and stress are all factors which place young people at particular risk for initiating and fall to binge drinking. Much of the research evidence suggests that the 'binge' drinking culture, mainly associated with young adults, is particularly linked with crime and disorder (Fergusson Horwood and Lynskey, 1995: 90: 935–46).

The European School Survey Project on Alcohol and other Drugs (ESPAD) study (1999), Sedqa's main research tool, has shown that Maltese-15 year olds are in the same category as the Scandinavian-15 year olds when it comes to binge drinking (The Malta Independent on Sunday, January 16, 2005:23). Sedqa, the agency in Malta against drug and alcohol abuse has been co-coordinating locally since 1995. According to the ESPAD 2003 statistics released in December 2004, Malta has a high rate of binge drinking – 25% – when compared to other countries. In fact, Malta rates fifth after Ireland (32%), the Netherlands (28%), Isle of Man (27%) and United Kingdom (27%) (The Malta Independent on Sunday, January 16, 2005:23).

In general, schools with high bingeing rates, 34% of non-binge drinkers reported being insulted or humiliated by binge drinkers, 13% reported being pushed, hit or assaulted, 54% reported having to take care of a drunk student, 68% were interrupted while studying and 26% of women experienced an unwanted sexual advance (The Malta Independent on Sunday, January 16, 2005:23). This data however is not relative to the Malta situation.

Statistics of frequent alcohol deaths and rates of liver disease are a useful indicator of chronic health problems caused by excessive drinking. Spanish researchers have become concerned about alcohol drinking and are contemplating changes to the legislation, which regulates alcohol consumption by the young. There is evidence that the problem could even more serious in Malta (The Malta Independent on Sunday, January 16, 2005:23). However, statistics are not available and information is difficult to require.

2.4   Theoretical Perspectives

The perception of risk is an important factor in this research because it gives Maltese people a way of understanding how serious underage drinking is in terms of crime, mental disturbance and social disability. Otway and von Winfeldt (1982: 14: 247-56) argue that people's risk perception might be influenced by a number of 'negative hazard attributes'. Pidgeon (1992), in the Royal Society report, have extracted the following headings:

Involuntary exposure to risk - Young people tend to perceive that as they grow older, the risk for alcohol consumption decreases (Muscat, et al., 2002). Parents need to know that alcohol use can also be a warning sign or a cry for help, that something is seriously wrong in a child's life (The Sunday Times of Malta, Sunday, April 11, 2004:79). If parents, counsellors, or teachers, reach children early enough, they can intervene before troubling behaviours lead to serious emotional disturbances, alcohol consumption, illicit drug use, failure in school, family discord, violence, or even suicide.

Lack of personal control over outcome – It is common knowledge that underage drinking persists, despite their increased efforts, young people can obtain identification that falsely presents their age as 16. 'Although by Law, no alcohol should be served to young people under the age of 16, everybody knows that this is hardly ever observed, especially when it is difficult to tell whether one who claims to be 16 is in reality 15 or even 14. The Law, no matter how inadequate, should be strictly enforced. Sadly, one hardly hears of any bar owners being arraigned for serving alcohol to minors' (Department of Information, Malta, 2004a).

In the study conducted by Professor Vassallo (2004), as many as 86.7%, participants unhesitatingly confirm that such a Law should be introduced. 11% stated that it should not, while the remaining 2.3% did not give a definite answer. 81.3% of those in the 16-25-age bracket agree with its introduction. The highest percentage in its favour was registered among persons aged 36-50, a category that is generally burdened with the care of young people, with 89.5% expressing themselves in favour (The Sunday Times, November 14, 2004:6).

There is a connection between young people drinking and criminal behaviour. Fights outside bars probably result because of the high intake of alcohol, resulting in criminal behaviour. The police find it difficult to detect drinking activities when it occurs in a private setting, such as drinking at home, at a party, or during *festi* (The Sunday Times of Malta, Sunday, April 11, 2004:79). To enhance the problem of underage drinking in Malta exists, some pictures of young people drinking at the village *festi* were taken during the month of August and September 2004 (Appendix M). For ethical concerns, some of the pictures are shown blurred on purpose so that the persons in the pictures would not be identified.

Lack of personal experience with the risk - Young people may see alcohol as a way of keeping troubles at bay and fostering a feeling of security (Bezzina, Clark, and Borg, 1997). Young people may see the consumption of alcohol as a way of allowing oneself to explore other relationships, whilst providing opportunities to explore sexual relationships in a less threatening context, where drinking may be used to excuse one's behaviour.

Difficulty in managing risk exposure - Malta should have comprehensible Laws, which prohibit alcohol consumption for those under age (The Sunday Times of Malta, Sunday, April 11, 2004:79). The police task force should work hard to control the sale of alcohol to minors to safeguard the health and safety of young people. Small shops that sell alcohol should also be Law enforced, together with the clubs and bars in entertainment places.

Uncertainty about probabilities or consequences of exposure - In the study carried out by Professor Mario Vassallo, two questions were asked: (a) whether the owner of the locality in which the persons picked up by the police should be fined and (b) whether the individual caught should be fined (The Sunday Times, November 14, 2004:6). The study showed that 83.8% think the individual should be fined and 89.6% think that the owner or club where the individual is caught should also be fined. 15.4% of the respondents stated that the individual caught should not be fined (The Sunday Times, November 14, 2004:6).

2.5 Other Theoretical Perspectives

Other theories which relate to the development of young people and to the research being studied are namely the Cognitive-Developmental Perspective and Social Learning Theory.

2.5.1 Cognitive-Developmental Perspective

The cognitive-developmental approach stresses that 'as children become adults they change the way they see themselves and their world and that this change involves thinking processes' (Santrock, 1981). The main theorists outlining this approach are Jean Piaget and Laurence Kohlberg. Piaget believes that adolescents' development is the results of the interaction of biological and genetic factors and environmental experiences. He believes thinking occurs when an individual adapts to the experiences of the moment and reorganises past ways of thinking. An individual shapes his/her perceptions on past and present experiences. These may lead to both positive and negative effects, according to the experience the individual is facing.

2.5.2 Social Learning Theory

The Social Learning Theorists believe that 'we acquire a wide range of such behaviours, thoughts and feelings through observing others' behaviour; these observations form an important part of our development' (Santrock, 1993:63). Adults should give an example to young people regarding alcohol use in entertainment places and/or at home. The children of parents who drink frequently may also turn out to be the same. If children see their parents drink, or are even offered to drink, then they perceive that drinking is not harmful because 'our' parents drink.

2.6 The concept of underage drinking

The concept of underage drinking is linked to a specific prohibition, namely the consumption of alcohol by individuals who are below culturally or legally defined threshold (Heath, 2000: 145). Underage alcohol use is a problem because it is more likely to kill young people than all illegal drugs combined (Young, et al., 2002: 68(3): 309–322). This could be one of the main reasons why International Governments prohibit underage drinking and the purchase of alcohol by minors. In the United States underage drinking is a serious public health problem and it is associated with lower educational attainment, greater likelihood of attempting suicide or of engaging in risky sexual behaviour and increased risk of drinking-driving mortality compared with the population 21 years and older' (Primedia Company, 2004). Where Malta is concerned, no data is available about young people and alcohol mortality.

During the transition between childhood and adulthood, significant changes occur in the body, including rapid hormonal alterations and the formation of new networks in the brain (Spear, 2002: (14): 71–81). Exposing the brain to alcohol during this period may interrupt key processes of brain development, possibly leading to mild cognitive impairment as well as to further escalation of drinking (Spear, 2002: (14): 71–81).

According to findings of a new study, released by the Substance Abuse and Mental Health Services Administration (SAMHSA), young people, age 12 to 17, who use alcohol, are more likely to report behavioural problems, especially aggressive, delinquent, and criminal behaviours (NIAAA, 2002). Some evidence indicates that genetic factors may also contribute to the relationship between early drinking and subsequent alcoholism (Virkkunen, et al., 1997: 173–189).

Thirteen to fifteen year-olds are at high risk to begin drinking (Johnston, et al., 1995). An American study indicates that those who began drinking before age 14 were 11 times more likely to have ever been in a fight while drinking or after drinking than adults who began drinking after the age of 21 (Hingson, et al., 2001: 108(4): 872-877). Those who start drinking before age 14 are 12 times more likely to increase the risk of alcohol related injury while under the influence of alcohol sometime in their life (Young, et al., 2002: 309–322). Young people who begin drinking before age 15 are four times more likely to develop alcohol dependence at some time in their lives compared with those who have their first drink at age 20 or older (Grant, et al., 1997).

From these studies we learn that the younger a person begins to drink, the greater the chance he or she will develop a problem with alcohol later in life. All of these problems are magnified by early onset of underage drinking. Delaying the age onset of alcohol use may improve the chance that young people will be safe, healthy and Law abiding. According to Grant, et al., 1997, if drinking is delayed until age 21, a child's risk of serious alcohol related problems will be decreased by 70 %.

2.6.1 Underage drinking and sexual behaviour

Alcohol is a depressant and numbs the nerve endings in both male and female genitalia (Doweiko, 1990). Alcohol also decreases normal hormone levels (Doweiko, 1990) and negatively affects the immune system (Rowell, 1997). Surveys of adolescents suggest that alcohol use is associated with risky sexual behavior and increased vulnerability to coercive sexual activity. Young people who drink are more likely than engage in sexual intercourse at an earlier age and with more partners (Bailey, et al., 1999). Amongst young people surveyed in New Zealand, alcohol misuse was significantly associated with unprotected intercourse and sexual activity before the age 16 (Fergusson, et al., 1996b: 98(1): 91-96).

About 44% of sexually active Massachusetts's young people said they were more likely to have sexual intercourse if they had been drinking and 17% said they were less likely to use contraceptives after drinking (Strunin, et al., 1992: 27(2): 129-146). Young girls who drink are more likely to have unprotected sex than girls who do not drink alcohol. Alcohol use in young people therefore is a strong predictor of both sexual activity and unprotected sex.

2.6.2 Underage drinking and children of alcoholics

Children of alcoholics are significantly more likely to initiate drinking during adolescence and to develop alcoholism than children of nonalcoholic parents (Cotton, 1979: 40:89-116). Environmental factors may also be involved, especially in alcoholic families, where children may start drinking earlier because of easier access to alcohol in the home, family acceptance of drinking and lack of parental monitoring. Harsh, inconsistent discipline and hostility or rejection toward children has also been found to significantly predict adolescent drinking and alcohol-related problems (Dawson, 2000: 61(5): 637–646).

School-aged children of alcoholic parents often have academic problems (Knop, et al., 1985: 46(4): 273-278) and appear to be at greater risk for delinquency and school truancy (Schuckit, et al., 1978: 166(3): 165-176). Teachers have rated children of alcoholics as significantly more overactive and impulsive than children of non-alcoholics. In one study, Brown and colleagues (Brown, et al., 2000) evaluated short–term memory skills in alcohol–dependent and nondependent adolescents ages 15 to 16 and found that young people with alcohol problems have a shorter-term memory.

Research also suggests that, children are less likely to drink when their parents are involved in their lives and when both parents and children report feeling close to each other (Moos and Billings, 1982 (7): 155-163). Children who are warned about alcohol by their parents may be less likely to start drinking.

2.7   Teenage alcohol use in Malta

According to the European School Project on Alcohol and Drugs (ESPAD) study, children in Malta seem to be exposed to alcohol quite early in their lives. Many young people are exposed to alcohol; however, few develop the patterns of drinking that lead to problematic drinking and alcohol dependence. The ESPAD 1995 Survey across country results that, Maltese 16 year olds top the list of alcohol consumption (Hibbell, et al., 1997). However, the ESPAD team did not indicate what factors could cause young people to misuse alcohol or whether it is possible to bring about changes in drinking culture to reduce the harm from alcohol misuse. It could have been wise for example if ESPAD suggested what could be done to align the interest of pubs and retailers with the objective of encouraging young people to enjoy drinking sensibly.

In Malta, during 1995, the ESPAD study reported that a high percentage of 16 year old Maltese adolescents use alcohol regularly (Bezzina, et al., 1997). Of the total number of respondents (n= 2832), 91.9% reported having used alcohol. 50% reported taking alcohol on 20 or more occasions in their life. Only 8% stated that they never consumed alcohol. Meanwhile, 44.3% reported having been drunk on at least one occasion in their life.

A notable 41.3% of the total number of respondents reported drinking wine before the age of 11 whereas 32.7% reported drinking beer at the same age (Bezzina, et al., 1997). These observations are sustained by data derived from the 1995 household census (Central Office of Statistics, 1998). The census results show that alcohol use is encouraged through the home environment at a very young age. This is because parents might be teaching young people what to drink and how much, so that when they go out with friends they would not exaggerate. There might be some speculations saying that parents are putting their children at risk.

Regular consumption of at least one unit (glass) of wine weekly was reported for 4% of children aged 0 to 4 years. In 1997 another project was held in Malta by the European School

Project on Alcohol and Drugs (ESPAD) and discovered a nearly 3% increase from the year of 1995 in the numbers reporting alcohol consumption (Muscat, et al., 2002).

In the ESPAD survey, 51% of those who had consumed alcohol (59% boys, 45% girls) reported doing so on 20 or more occasions in their lives. Boys were found out to be twice more likely to be heavier drinkers than girls. The survey has also revealed that there was a significant increase in the number of respondents – from 16.4% to 32.2% – who reported they consumed alcohol in a disco (The Times of Malta, December 15, 2004a: 18).

Many parents in Malta want the legal drinking age to be raised to 18 (Department of Information, Malta, 2004b). The study conducted by Professor Mario Vassallo (2004), among a representative sample of 300 Maltese, people were asked to indicate the age the Law should apply to, a range from 13-21 years was given. The two ages most frequently mentioned were 16, given by 35% of all the respondents, and 18, given by 54.6%. Strikingly again, 41% of young people aged 16-25 gave 16 as the age when the provision should be applicable, while another 48.7% from the same young people age group gave 18 as the age when this should be applicable (The Sunday Times, November 14, 2004:6).

Participants in this survey were asked whether they thought it should be possible for minors to buy alcohol from bars, retail outlets such as groceries and from supermarkets. As many as 98% stated that alcohol should definitely not be available to minors through bars, another 98% stated that it should not be available through retail outlets, while 97% said that it should not be available from supermarkets (The Sunday Times, November 14, 2004:6). These findings very clearly point to the need for a radical departure from current practices and the enforcement of any existing regulation that prevents minors from having access to alcohol.

Dr. George Grech, the Sedqa clinical director in 1998 (Malta Critique, 1998) argued that young people in Malta are highly exposed to alcohol drinking. This is because adults are violating the Law by promoting alcohol drinking to minors. One needs to take into consideration that the Law in Malta only prohibits underage drinking and selling or giving alcohol to minors and regulates the entry of young people under the age of 16 into entertainment establishments. It does not regulate alcohol consumption by minors. The Maltese Law and the Legal system are illustrated in section 2.8.1.

In Malta there are no actual services designed for young abusers as such, in the field neither of prevention, nor of treatment. The only services, which are available to young people in Malta, are Sedqa, Caritas and Alcoholics Anonymous (all found on World Wide Web). For this reason, that illicit abuse of drugs in Malta is recognised as a national problem and that Maltese are less tolerant towards use of illegal drugs. The majority of people population does not consider alcohol to be a drug, for the reason that alcohol is a legal substance, and that alcohol consumption provides positive effects such as stimulation or pleasure, with the least or non-existent toxic aftermath.

2.8   The Legal drinking age

The legal drinking age for different countries varies dramatically, from 0 to 21, as shown in Appendix E. At least 18 countries have a minimum drinking age of 18. Four countries have a national minimum age of 21: Egypt, Honduras, Samoa and the US. Three Canadian provinces set a minimum age of 18, the rest of provinces, the age of 19. In Japan, the minimum age is 20 whilst in Italy and Malta, 16. In countries such as Switzerland, young people can legally purchase alcohol at the age of 14. Some countries, including Greece and Indonesia, legislate the legal drinking of alcohol but are indifferent to alcohol consumption (International Centre for Alcohol Policies, 2004).

2.8.1   Maltese Law and the Legal System

It is illegal to sell alcohol to someone under the age of 16 in Malta. In the Maltese Code of Police Laws, a provision exists for the regulation of entry of young people under the age of 16 into entertainment establishments (Legal Malta, 2003).

The Maltese Law on the Maintenance of good order at places of entertainment, subsidiary Legislation 10.40 Article 6, states that:

(1) 'Persons under the age of sixteen shall not be allowed inside a place of entertainment, and young persons over the age of sixteen years shall, prior to admission to any such place, produce and show their identity card to the proprietor'.

(2) 'The proprietor shall be responsible to ensure that no person under the age of sixteen is allowed inside the place of entertainment'.

(3) 'Sub-regulation (1) of this regulation shall be reproduced on the admission ticket to any place of entertainment and any such ticket shall state that the holder shall only be admitted upon the production of his identity card or other document evidencing his identity'.

(4) 'Where any person under the age of sixteen people is found at a place of entertainment, the proprietor of the place of entertainment shall be guilty of an offence and shall, on conviction, be liable to the punishment of a fine (*multa*) of one hundred Maltese Liri (equiv. £ 160) for every such person in addition to other punishments specified under these Regulations' (Legal Malta, 2003).

The Maltese Law on the Shops for the sale of wine, beer, or spirituous liquors (Licences, good order and public decorum) regulations subsidiary Legislation 10.09 states that:

'It shall not be Lawful for any person holding a licence under these Regulations to allow any child under sixteen years of age to enter or loiter at the entrance of any bar or other premises where barmaids or artistes are employed; nor shall it be Lawful for any such child to enter or loiter at the entrance of any such bar or premises or to infringe any order given by any member of the Police Force to quit the neighbourhood thereof' (Legal Malta, 2003).

According to Social Solidarity Minister Dolores Cristina (The Times of Malta, December 15, 2004b: 1), in Malta there is no Law which prohibits young people under the age of sixteen people from drinking alcohol. Minister Ms. Cristina pointed out that the Maltese legislation only banned the sale of alcohol to children but did not prohibit consumption (The Times of Malta, December 15, 2004b: 1). One cannot understand why the Law in Malta penalises some who sells alcohol but not a person (underage) to buy alcohol. This could lead our young people having the 'Childhood' being prolonged unnecessarily. The Minister Ms. Cristina argued that the Government of Malta was working on the formulation of a national alcohol policy, which would lay emphasis on reaching out to parents and support services for abusers (The Times of Malta, December 15, 2004a: 18).

2.8.2   *U.K. and International Laws*

Under British Laws, children of any age can go into sections of pubs that are set aside for meals or as family rooms. Young people over 14 can go into pubs unaccompanied but cannot be served alcohol. Young people of 16 year-olds can buy and drink beer or cider but not spirits if they are having a meal. In Northern Ireland, nobody under 18 can enter a pub. In the United Kingdom, underage drinking Laws are more clearly structured compared with the Laws of Malta. There are strict Laws governing alcohol consumption in the UK, which are found to be at Her Majesty's Stationary Office (HMSO) on World Wide Web, also found in the bibliography.

In most of the developed countries, Law prohibits underage drinking. Minimal Legal Drinking Age (MLDA) ranges from 16 years old to 21 years old (World Health Organization, 1999). Despite these Laws, many young people in the prohibited age range do drink alcohol and substantial percentages of them have already started excessive drinking (Fletcher, et al., 2000: 61(1), 81-84).

2.9 Conclusion

The origin and constitution of alcohol has been discussed in the literature review. The literature review opened the debate by discussing what alcohol is and from where it originally derived. The risk factors associated with this phenomenon including the context of underage drinking are various, namely health-related issues, economic issues and crime issues. The importance, nature and extent of underage alcohol use in Malta have also been examined in the study.

Underage alcohol use is a serious problem because it typically results in young peoples' health and crime problems whilst jeopardising others that frequent them. The research shows that young people misuse alcohol due to variety of factors such as pressure from school, parents, peers and other social reasons. The literature review has revealed that the younger a person begins to drink, the greater the chance to develop a problem with alcohol later in life.

The theoretical perspectives that assimilate the study have also been discussed, namely being people's risk perception on negative hazard attributes, cognitive developmental theory and social learning theory. It was also essential for the researcher to focus on Maltese and International Laws to understand better the interpretation and meaning of the Law. One should bear in question that the Maltese Legislation only forbids the sale of alcohol to children but does not make note of illegal consumption of the C_2H_5OH. Despite these Laws, many young people have already experienced intoxication early in their lives as demonstrated by the methodology performed in Maltese schools.

From the study, one may note the frequency of intoxication of young people and whether the authorities, including security services, have been involved. To be able to rest assure parents and young people's families, certain security measures need to be employed. Without these security measures, young people may continue to drink and endanger their lives and other peoples'.

Methodology

3.1 Introduction

The study examines the problem of underage alcohol use in Malta. It focuses on attitudes and experience of alcohol among 13-15 year olds and on the prevention strategies used to reduce this problem. A number of studies have been conducted worldwide to analyse the risk factors associated with underage drinking (Fergusson, et al., 1996; Hibell, et al., 1997; Fletcher, et al., 2000; National Institute on Alcohol Abuse and Alcoholism 2002/3; and Home Office, 2004).

From the literature review we have learned that the younger the person begins to drink, the greater the chance he or she will develop a problem with alcohol later in life. Studies in Malta have indicated a high self-reported use of alcohol among young people (Bezzina, et al, 1997; Central Office of Statistics, 1998; Muscat, et al., 2002; Grech, 2004). The researcher now aims to go beyond what have been studied in the past and learnt. The aim of the researcher is now to use the acquired knowledge and exchange it into an extend detailed case study.

3.2 The research tool

According to Kellner, et al., (1991) the choice of research tool depends on the properties of that tool and on the kind of research being conducted. In achieving the aims of the study, data was collected by distributing self-completion questionnaires, focus group discussions and observational sessions. The questionnaire was slightly amended after the pilot study was carried out. Although there were no radical problems with the data collection instruments, some slight adjustments were introduced, which are further explained in section 3.4.

3.3 Field procedure

Focus groups were conducted in respect of the 'reason' of drinking, its antecedents, expectations and potential consequences. Consequences involved respondents' concerns with their own safety, their possible involvement in antisocial behaviour and the social significance of their drinking, including sexual behaviour. The total number of young people participating in this research was 241, 99 (41%) were boys and 142 (59%) were girls. The research also involved another 16 young people in the pilot study.

Approvals from the Head of the Education Division in Malta were obtained before the study actually took place. The researcher visited the Guidance and Counselling Personnel of each school, taking part in the study before the questionnaires were distributed and explained procedures to teachers who were willing to supervise the surveys. Teachers were asked not to help students in the questionnaire whilst at the same time, assuring students of their anonymity in the questionnaire.

The researcher read the instructions to all students participating in the research before administration of the questionnaires. The same instructions were shown on the first page of the questionnaire, which explained the scope of the survey. Teachers could only help students in the general understanding of the questions within the questionnaire. Students were informed of the survey at the beginning of the lesson and were told that the study was on alcohol drinking. After completion of the questionnaire, the papers were collected and were placed in the envelope, sealed and deposited in the respective head teacher's office. These in turn were handed to the researcher.

3.4   The pilot study

A pilot study was conducted concerning the questionnaires. 'Piloting is essentially concerned with identifying any deficiencies in the design of a questionnaire such as problems in the administration of the questionnaire or the changes in the phrasing and sequence of questions' (Scarman Centre, 2001b (3): 6-40). The researcher used the pilot study technique to ensure that the instructions and guidelines were clear and to assess whether the questions to be asked made sense and were set in an appropriate manner. The family members were also given the questionnaire as part of the pilot study.

Two days before the pilot study, participants were all contacted by telephone individually. The young people involved in the pilot study were excluded from the main one. The pilot study was held on 27 December 2004. Sixteen students (16 years and under) participated enthusiastically and expressed sincere willingness to participate. The researcher together with all participants chose a quiet restaurant for a proper venue. The designation of the questionnaire was pre-tested in the pilot study. The main points that emerged from the pilot study were: the questionnaire appeared to be of proper length for completion (i.e. thirty questions to be answered in 20 minutes), but eleven pages appeared to be a lot. Therefore, the researcher was encouraged to reduce the design of the questionnaire to three pages as presenting many pages was uneconomical. Copies of the original questionnaire and of the pilot study are presented in appendix F.

After the pilot study, the questionnaire was modified to take the form of a multiple-choice question and answer, where the answer required was just ticking the particular box. This reduce the amount of writing in the questionnaire, thus helping in reducing the time needed to complete the questionnaire and any problems encountered by the students as regards illiteracy. At the same time made it easier to review and draw conclusions. Some questions were rearranged in an appropriate sequence (refer to the original questionnaire). Question 1 to 4 of the questionnaire remained unchanged. Question 5: *'Do you go out at weekends?'* was changed with *'Till what time do you normally stay out with friends?'* as youngsters do normally go out at weekends and it was more important to establish how long they normally stay out especially with friends. Question 6 of the questionnaire, another column was added for the *'never'* option. In question 7 and 9 the *'centilitres'* from the choice options were removed, as not everyone acknowledges the volume of alcohol and the volumes mentioned in these questions were rearranged according to the volume of alcohol a normal person consumes. Question 8, 10 and 12 remained unchanged.

Question 11 was changed to *'How much do you drink on a night out?'* as this could have given an indication of binge drinking amongst young people. In the pilot study, students were also asked to mention three to five clubs in Paceville that are most popular amongst teenagers. In the main study, question 13 was set up differently. Students were requested to mention few clubs in Paceville instead of three, so one may gather where alcohol is more promoted to young people. Question 14 has been altered slightly so that the reader may understand it better. Question 15 remained unchanged. Question 16 was rearranged to see what youngsters think of a person who does not drink alcohol and does not go to Paceville. Question 17 to 30 remained unchanged.

3.5   Surveys in schools

A survey is known as 'a system for collecting information to describe, compare, or explain knowledge, attitudes and behaviour. Surveys involve setting objectives for information collection, designing research, preparing a reliable and valid data collection instrument, administering and scoring the instrument, analysing the data and reporting the results' (Fink 1995:1).

The surveys were carried out in State and Non-State Secondary schools. The researcher attempted to include all students born in 1989, 1990 and 1991, that is, having ages from 13 to 15 years. Students, who attended school on the days the surveys were conducted, all participated.

3.6   The use of questionnaires

The researcher ensured that the questions in the questionnaire were numbered, well printed and easy to read. The researcher also ensured that there was no ambiguity within the questions, which were highlighted in the pilot study.

The researcher chose to use questionnaires because this method offers flexibility and broadness of scope and it is inexpensive technique. By using a questionnaire, a more geographically diverse sample may be obtained, thus resulting in more widely collected opinions. The interpretation of data may be time consuming; however, this was reduced by the introduction of more closed-ended questions rather than open-ended questions. Closed-ended questions involved ticking of small boxes, placed next to the statements to answer. If the students did not understand a question, the researcher was present together with the teacher of the classroom, to clarify any queries. Open-ended questions were given where the researcher wanted to find out the names of clubs that young people frequent.

The main advantage of using the questionnaire in this study was to collect the information more quickly, whilst the main disadvantages were that students might not have wished to reveal the information or they might have thought that the clubs in Paceville will close because of their answering truthfully.

Another problem with questionnaires was that some participants did not fill in the questionnaire completely, or failed to understand the questions well, as ensued in this research.   Some students failed to express their views in English so some of them answered the questionnaire in Maltese.   Another problem with questionnaires is that of verbal and communication problems. Those questionnaires which were not wholly completed were still used for data analysis even those questionnaires which were completed in Maltese. After the study, all questionnaires have been discarded.

3.7   Group discussions and Focus group

Group discussions and focus group are 'a small number of individuals, brought together as a discussion or resource group, are more valuable many times over than any representative sample. They are not simply discussion groups but are designed to generate ideas and encourage interplay of thoughts and reflections' (Flick, 1998:116).   The researcher chose Focus/Discussion groups to give students the opportunity to air their views. It was also however taken into consideration that group discussion participants could have been less honest or even prone to exaggerate due to the group dynamic. 'Such a group, discussing collectively their sphere of life and probing into it as they meet one another's disagreements, will do more to lift the veils covering the sphere of life ...' (Flick, 1998:116).

The target number of individual interviews following each focus group was 6.   There were 24 mixed participants in total from each school (boys and girls) who took part and shared their experiences with the researcher.   The researcher led the group and guided the discussion amongst the participants.   Focus group sessions took between one to two hours and all records were documented with notes.   By using this method, the researcher encouraged the exploration of ideas and interpretation of what young people say.   The researcher did not impose on any participant to take part in the discussion.

3.8   Observational methods

'...Watching is certainly an important part of collecting data in the field setting...' (Bailey, 1999). Observation methods have also been used in the study to explore the attitudes and behaviour associated with young people.   The researcher has chosen to use the observation technique as a method to gain information, which would may not be collected or learned through the discussion or questionnaire alone. By using observational methods, the researcher did not have to ask people about their behaviours and action of others (DePoy, et al., 1998: 219-221).

Observational sessions were conducted during the Christmas holidays from school. In this way, young people find an opportunity to meet their friends, go out and may stay out late because there is no school. The researcher has made nine of two hours duration. Three clubs were observed during the observational sessions and each club was visited three times on average.

The observation periods were divided into three phases: early in the evening to midnight, midnight to early in the morning and late in the evening, early in the morning.

The researcher has attempted to focus on the physical and social environments, young people, bar and security staff, drinking patterns, antisocial behaviour, the total environment of drinking in Paceville and the lack of control by security and the police. The physical layout, the attitudes and behaviour of young people and social atmosphere have also been observed during the observational sessions. The researcher planned to observe warning signs inside pubs, clubs and discothèques concerning alcohol abuse and whether door supervisors ask for the proof-of-age cards when young, people visit discothèques, clubs and pubs. The researcher has also planned to observe the number of young people who will be let into places of entertainment and given alcoholic drinks.

Non-participant observation was used in this research to obtain an understanding of a natural context without the influence of the observer. 'Non-Participant observation, where the observer is, in effect, an eavesdropper, someone who attempts to observe people without interacting with them and typically, without their knowing that they are being observed (Scarman, 2001c (3): 6-6). By using observational methods, there might have been the risk of misrepresentation of typical events and behaviours of young people, because the presence of the researcher may have caused the participants to vary their actions.

Observational methods alone are quite unreliable because the researcher may miss an event of interest occurring at the bar, whilst viewing the other end of the hall. In order to remain unnoticed, the researcher had to participate in the lively events of the club, such as talking to others and dancing. Observational notes were used, in order to maximise the observation of young people in the club. In order to reduce the number of actions of interest missed, the clubs were frequented often, but at different times. Details of the observation are discussed in Chapter 4, Section III.

3.9   Reliability and Validity

Reliability refers to the likelihood that a given measurement procedure will yield the same description of a given phenomenon if that measurement is repeated whilst validity refers to the extent to which a specific measurement provides data that measure what it is intended to measure (University of Minnesota, 2005).

Adjustments in the survey methodology were designed to ensure the maximum possible reliability in the responses. The main objective of the researcher was to gather information with regards to the attitude of young people aged 13-15 towards alcohol consumption. The researcher also wanted to know the quantity of alcohol young people consume. The aims and characteristics of alcohol consumption amongst young people in ESPAD (1995, 1997) surveys are consistent with the study, thereby supporting the reliability and validity of the data collection used in this study. The design of the questionnaire however was adapted to the research being studied and has been tested in the pilot study.

3.10   Analysis of data

The purpose of the data analysis phase is to explain the underlying patterns and the relationships of the data obtained (Talbot, 1995). Following consultation with a statistician, it has been established that regression analysis will be the main statistical tool to be used. The data has been analysed by means of a programme supporting statistical analysis namely and by the use of tables and graphs.

3.11   Ethical considerations

Ethics are generally defined as a set of moral standards by which people regulate their behaviour. Barnes, (1979) goes further when he defines ethics as factors, which '…arise when we try to decide between one course of action and another, not in terms of expediency or efficiency but by reference to standards of what is morally right or wrong'.

The researcher tried to work within the confines of current legislation over matters such as intellectual property including copyright, trademark, patents, privacy and confidentiality, data protection and human rights. The researcher has made use of the existing professional associations in which devised his or her own code of ethics such as the British Psychological Association (BPA) and the Social research association (SRA) which are found on World Wide Web.

The following ethical considerations were considered and tackled in this study:

- **Anonymity**, which involves keeping the identity of each person secret, was achieved by not recording any information that may allow young people to be traced individually or as a group.

- **Confidentiality**, whereby any information obtained about young people during the study was maintained as secret. The researcher was bound not to reveal any information obtained during the data collection to anyone. The results during the data collection were kept in a secure place and used only for this study.

The researcher ensured anonymity and confidentiality by explaining that the survey was voluntary (a statement was shown in the introduction of the questionnaire, which supported this assertion) and ensured that the questionnaires will be disposed of at the end of the project. The researcher granted the research participants the opportunity to ask questions about any aspect of the research, at any time during or exactly after their participation in the research.

The researcher ensured the *benevolence* of each individual by safeguarding the physical, social, and psychological wellbeing. The researcher also ensured that the individual is not adversely affected (*non-maleficience*) by participation in the research itself. The research being studied was undertaken to the highest possible methodological standard wherever possible and that the findings are reported accurately and truthfully in such a way that the rights and integrity of every individual is presented (Bulmer, 1982).

All participants in this research were given respect and a fair treatment (*justice*) by assuring them that no favouritism or discrimination would take place. The author introduced himself to the participants and presented them with a letter from University of Leicester stating that the author himself is currently studying for an M.Sc. in Security and Risk Management from Leicester University on the research of Risk perception, awareness and prevention measures to reduce underage drinking and the illegal purchase of alcohol in Malta'. A brief introduction was made to what the study was all about (Bulmer, 1982).

3.12 Problems, limitations and conclusion

The first limitation of the study was that the response categories on the questionnaire were not exhaustive; some answers were very limited and were written according to the understanding of the participant. Although a great number of students were selected as the target population (241), the data may not be representative of the total student population. It was difficult to select a sample from a classroom because the researcher did not know the students and who would voice different opinions.

Another problem was a language problem. This included the possibility that not every question was read with care, thus resulting in bias and incorrect representation of the answer. The questionnaire might not been wholly completed due to various reasons, namely the participant being in a hurry to complete the questionnaire, or randomly picking an answer.

This chapter described the research methods and tool used for the data collection. Chapter 4 demonstrates the presentation and analysis of the data collected.

Data Chapters

SECTION I

4.1   Introduction

This chapter is divided into three sections. The first provides information on the level of co-operation of the participating schools and students, the student's level of comprehension of the questionnaire and the data analysis, which resulted from the survey. The second section provides information on focus group session and the third part discusses information reported during the observation methodology.

4.2   School and Student Cooperation

During the Christmas Season 2004, the questionnaires were distributed amongst students between the 13-15 year bracket, in State and Non-State schools. Four schools in total participated in the study, two State schools, and two Non-State schools. Students from these schools took the opportunity to share their attitudes, behaviour, and experience towards alcohol use amongst young people.

All students within the age bracket present at school took part in the survey. They did this in the presence of their teacher and the researcher as stated in chapter 3. Out of 241 males and females born in 1989, 1990, 1991, there were 99 (41%) boys and 142 (59%) girls who contributed and voluntarily participated in the study.

4.3   Prevalence of alcohol use among 13 to 15 year olds, 2004

A high percentage of students reported alcohol consumption in their lifetime (Table 1). In fact 86% of the sample reported using alcohol, 83% reported having used alcohol during the last 12 months and 68% report having used alcohol during the last 30 days.

When students were asked about the occasions where they may have been indulged in heavy drinking, 11% boys out of 99 participants, reported that they have never taken alcohol in their lifetime, 17% girls out of 142 participants, reported that they have never consumed alcohol in their lifetime. One may note that the young people who reported drinking more alcohol were less likely to report negative consequences and more likely to acknowledge the positive aspects of alcohol consumption.

Table 1

Frequency of alcohol use amongst students 13-15 years old – Males and Females

Number of times	0	1-2	3-5	6-9	10-19	20-39	40 or more
In your lifetime							
13 years	6%	2%	4%	6%	1%	3%	1%
14 years	6%	5%	3%	3%	6%	4%	8%
15 years	2%	2%	4%	4%	6%	6%	18%
Total	**14%**	**9%**	**11%**	**13%**	**13%**	**13%**	**27%**
During the last 12 months							
13 years	8%	3%	3%	3%	4%	1%	0%
14 years	5%	6%	5%	5%	5%	4%	4%
15 years	4%	5%	7%	5%	7%	9%	6%
Total	**17%**	**14%**	**15%**	**13%**	**16%**	**14%**	**10%**
During the last 30 days							
13 years	11%	6%	1%	2%	1%	0%	0%
14 years	11%	9%	6%	6%	2%	1%	1%
15 years	10%	11%	7%	6%	2%	6%	1%
Total	**32%**	**26%**	**14%**	**14%**	**5%**	**7%**	**2%**

4.4 Alcohol consumption

Table 2 below, presents data relating to the quantity of alcohol consumed during the participant's last drinking occasion. 15% of the boys reported drinking less than a regular bottle or can of beer and 12% reported drinking 6 or more regular bottles or cans of beer. Girls seem not to drink beer as much as boys do. 20% of the girls reported drinking less than a regular bottle or can of beer. Only 1% of girls reported drinking 6 or more regular bottles or cans of beer.

With regards to the consumption of spirits, the girls drank more than the boys. In fact, there were 11% of the girls reported drinking liquor (5 drinks or more). With regards to wine, boys seem to drink more than girls. 9% of the boys reported drinking a bottle of wine or more. Overall, the most widely used beverages amongst students participating in this study were beer followed by liquor and wine.

In relation to the quantities of alcohol consumed at the last drinking occasion, it was interesting to note the differences (Appendix G, Table A1), which emerged between both sexes. Males prefer to consume more beer and wine whilst females prefer to drink more spirit. The study has brought out a clear tendency for males to report consuming larger quantities and more often. It is also clear that there is a tendency for males to start drinking at an earlier age and to indulge in more excessive drinking than females.

4.5   The first use of alcohol

The age at which alcohol is first consumed is often regarded as a good summary measure of the changing trends in alcohol use, on the grounds that the earlier the age of initiation, the greater the likelihood of increased consumption, with the associated health and behavioral problems, during the development of young people.

As resulted from this study, young people seem to be exposed quite early to alcohol use (Table 2). 12 % reported drinking beer before the age 11, while 13 % reported drinking wine before age 11. The data from this survey indicates that the majority of respondents have been drinking alcohol by the age of 15 and that 3% have experienced drunkenness at the age of 10. One of the main reasons that young people are exposed to alcohol at a very young age is because alcohol is very well promoted at home (Central Office of Statistics, 1998). An example, which is worth to mention is a mother or the grandmother of the child who would suggest giving the baby a pacifier with wine so that the child sleeps well during the night without giving them any trouble. According to the researcher's belief, this is the first invitation to trouble.

Table 2

Alcohol consumption at first use – Males and Females

Age at first use	Never	10 years old or less	11 years old	12 years old	13 years old	14 years old	15 years old
Drink beer (at least one glass)	30%	12%	14%	15%	13%	12%	4%
Drink wine (at least one glass)	20%	13%	14%	17%	18%	13%	5%
Get drunk on alcohol	65%	3%	1%	2%	9%	10%	10%

Although most students reported not drinking heavily, it is important to note that, a small percentage of young people drink heavily. The chart (Figure 1) demonstrates the frequency when young people get drunk. Whilst 71 % report never have been drunk on at least one occasion or more, 17 % reported getting drunk on at least one to two times, 11% reported having been drunk on at least three to five times. Only 1% of the group reported being drunk at least six to nine times. Not all the students may have said the truth as not every one would admit that someday he/she might have got drunk. The reasons for not telling the truth could have been that they were afraid or they did not want to remember what they have been through.

Figure 1

Students 13-15 who got drunk on alcohol in their lifetime

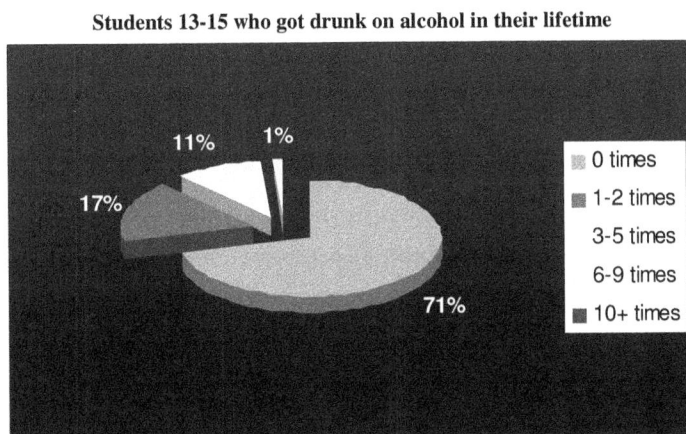

4.6   Drinking Venues

From the data (Appendix H, Table A2), the most popular drinking venues for boys were at a disco or nightclub 63%, in a restaurant 55%, followed by pubs or bars 51%. For girls the most popular drinking venues were discos or nightclubs 49%, in a pub or bar 42%, followed by in a restaurant 32%. This is a good indication, which shows that young people illegally are allowed inside a place of entertainment.

4.7   The Illegal Purchase of Alcohol in Malta

While it is illegal to sell alcohol to a young person who is under the age of 16, it must be noted that a number of participants in the study claim obtaining their alcoholic beverages from discos or nightclubs, pubs, bars and restaurants. It seems that retailers cannot understand that they can be held responsible for injuries or damages that may occur to young people because of alcohol. If the Law in Malta is to be enforced, the Law may hold adults including retailers responsible for the health, safety, and behaviour of minors. However, at this stage, no Laws are strictly enforced so young people resort to drinking and retailers ascertain themselves by keeping on flaunting the Law.

4.8   Attitudes towards alcohol consumption

Amongst the Maltese sample, students have shown a sound knowledge of the possible negative effects of alcohol abuse. Many agreed that alcohol consumption might bring negative effects and cited that an important reason for not drinking is that it may lead to serious accidents and that it is bad for one's health. Others reported the problems they experienced because of alcohol use, were mainly interpersonal rather than sexual or criminal.

The main problems reported were problems in relationships with parents, quarrels or argument problems in relationships with friends, damage to objects or clothes and scuffles or fights. The participants also referred to positive consequences, they felt more friendly, outgoing and happy when they drank alcohol. The most frequently recorded negative consequences included feeling sick, harming one's health and doing something one would regret.

Unplanned and unprotected sex was not readily recognized or spontaneously listed as a problem. However, when the issue was raised, many acknowledged they had been in situations, which risked leading to unprotected sex. One may find it difficult to believe that people at 13 years perform sexual activities at such a young age, as found out in this study. Moreover, performing sexual activities after drinking, leads to unknowledgeable actions, for example disorientation of the surroundings, accepting sex with an unrecognized partner, finding one's self sleeping outside and waking up totally oblivious to the state and surroundings of the individual.

4.9   Drinking Perceptions

There seems to be a tendency for males to report drinking on more occasions than females. With regard to lifetime use, while 11% of males reported drinking on more than 40 occasions in a lifetime, 9% of females report doing so (Appendix I, Table A3). The same trends can be observed with frequency of alcohol use in the last 12 months.

4.9.1 *Perceived consequences of drinking*

Those young people who reported drinking more were likely to acknowledge positive outcomes: feel relaxed, feel happy, forget problems and feel more friendly and outgoing. On the other hand, the same cohort was less likely to report the following negative consequences: mixing with drugs, get into trouble with police, getting into fights or causing trouble.

4.10 Information on Sedqa and Caritas

In Question 27 of the questionnaire, students were asked about Sedqa and Caritas, two from very few organizations that offer services for people with alcoholic and drug problems. It was the researcher's intention to test their knowledge on what they know and feel about these agencies, how aware they are about the programmes/services that they offer and what benefit they provide for the society. Students 13 to 15 year old, boys and girls reported as follows.

One third of the students said that they know nothing or little about Sedqa and Caritas whilst two thirds of the students reported that these organizations help people stay away from the abuse of alcohol and drugs and drive away peoples' bad habits. In general, Sedqa and Caritas have been described by students as preachers and/or rehabilitators that raise public awareness on the serious consequences of alcohol misuse and drug abuse.

Five boys reported that Sedqa and Caritas do not help at all, as they report alcohol incidents to the police. Others wrote insolent phrases against the organisations. Some of the answers in the questionnaire were probably honest, indicating that young people are tired of Sedqa and Caritas. Some students indicated that these two organisations work only to ban alcohol from young people's lives, which according to the researcher is not a correct statement.

4.11 Reasons for not drinking

The research analysis highlights the reasons why people should abstain from drinking. The data revealed that young people who drink are less bound by religious, societal and familial bonds and are not frightened by the possible negative personal and social effects derived from drinking. Students disagree that alcohol tastes horrible and that drinking is against their principles. The only difference across these stages was that both drinkers and non-drinkers acknowledged that drinking is bad for health. They also both agreed that people who drink lose control in an unpleasant way and the habit is likely to have bad effects on family life. A small percentage of students acknowledged that drinking becomes a habit; it costs too much and makes one put on weight.

4.12 Future drinking

In question 21, students were asked if they think they will be drinking alcohol when they are 25 years old. The behaviour related to all students and to both sexes reported as follows. Male respondents, that is, 49% did not know if they would be drinking when they are older, whilst 45% of females said they did not know. Only 13% of the boys and 8% of the girls stated that they would not be drinking alcohol at all. However, 38% boys and 47% girls said they would be drinking alcohol when they are 25. One can predict that by the age of twenty-five girls are likely to drink alcohol more than boys are. This is a good indication for the Government of Malta to start implementing effective strategies in order to reduce underage drinking in Malta.

Young people are also more likely to see themselves drinking alcohol later on in life and to estimate that their friends also drink alcohol. One could interpret these responses in a number of ways. It may be that the young people in the sample are actually less aware than those who are not drinking. Another interpretation could be that although they are aware of the negative effects of alcohol consumption, the fact that they are drinking creates the need to justify their behaviour. At the same time, the researcher emphasizes that one should not draw hasty conclusions given the limited data available.

4.13 Reasons for students to drink alcohol

In Question 20, students were asked the reason for drinking alcohol. Indications (Table 3) show that there was a high percentage on those who drink alcohol because they wanted to feel good (36%) followed by knowing that it is harmful but they do not care (17%) and to forget problems (16%).

Table 3

Reasons for students to drink alcohol

Reasons for drinking alcohol	BOYS Number of participants 99 (41%)	GIRLS Number of participants 142 (59%)
I want to feel good	44 (44%)	42 (30%)
I do not want to stand out from the group	13 (13%)	6 (4%)
I have nothing else to do	11 (11%)	7 (5%)
I want to forget my problems	21 (21%)	17 (12%)
I want to be like my friends	12 (12%)	17 (12%)
I know that it is harmful but I don't care	18 (18%)	22 (15%)

4.14   Risk Awareness

A high level of awareness of the negative effects of alcohol use has been reported in the study. However, one notes a gross discrepancy between awareness and actual behaviour. So while young people are reporting a high level of awareness, they are still drinking. In addition, while a large percentage reported awareness of negative effects of alcohol use their knowledge seems to be likely limited. The question exploring anticipated drinking behaviour substantiates this argument since 48% boys and 45% girls did not know whether they would be drinking when they are older. 7% of the students did not answer the question. Question 19 revealed that all students normally drink with family members and friends.

4.15   Adults buying alcohol for minors

With regards to question 24, students were asked whether during the last three years, any adult has bought alcohol for them. If the answer to question 24 was a 'yes', question 25 requested students to mention the person involved. If the answer was a 'no', students had the option to leave question 25 blank. The data (Figure 2) however revealed that there is a high percentage of 15-year-old boys (28%) and 15 year-old girls (17%), who reported adults buying alcohol for them during the last three years.

Figure 2

The Illegal Purchase of Alcohol to minors during the last three years

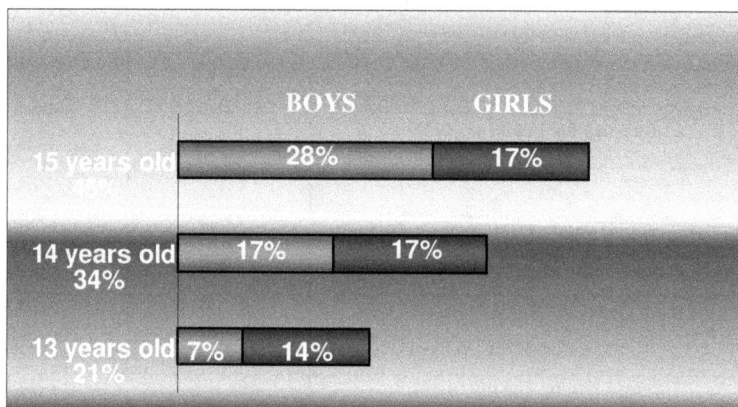

4.16   Alcohol and Aggressiveness

In question 26, students were requested to indicate if they knew any relatives or friends who after drinking alcohol acted aggressively. The data revealed that 24% of the students have relatives or friends who after drinking alcohol act aggressively, whereas 66% answered that they do not have friends or relatives who engage in aggressiveness after drinking alcohol. These young people may perceive that they will not act aggressively after drinking alcohol simply because their families or friends do the same and nothing happens. 10% of participants did not comment. Virtually, 15-year-old students agreed that boys react more aggressively than girls do. Very few students believe that those who are under the age of sixteen should be given lighter drinks.

4.17   Use and academic performance

In question 2, (Appendix J, Table A4), students were requested to grade their performance at school that is, from A - E (excellent – fairly good) to U (poor) and in question 3 (Appendix K, Table A5) students were requested to show the relationship that they had between themselves and their Parents / Legal Guardians at home. Those who drink and who have between fairly good and poor relationships at home tended to perceive their grade levels as being lower than those who do not drink.

When one considers alcohol consumption and academic performance, the responses indicate that those who perceive themselves as low achievers are drinking more. This could be interpreted either as an attempt by the respondent to alleviate low self esteem resulting from a feeling of failure within the school context, or the consumption of alcohol is in itself interfering with the general disposition toward education and school life. One may also conclude that these two variables are interacting to result in drinking behaviour patterns amongst young people.

4.18   Time out with friends and after school days

Students were asked in question 4 followed by question 5, whether they go out after school and how long would they normally stay out with friends. The majority of males and females (13 to 14 year olds) say that they do not normally go out after school whilst 15-year-old students reported going out after school. 13-year-old students normally stay out with friends between 8:00 p.m. and 1.00 a.m.   14-year-old students reported staying out with friends between 7:00 p.m. and 3.30 a.m.   The data also revealed that those at the age of 15 stay out with friends even later, with the time ranging between 10:00 p.m and 4:00 a.m.   It is noted that Bars and Clubs in Malta stay open all-night and early in the morning and close at around 4:00 to 5.00 a.m. One can conclude that that those at the age of 15 are more likely to be at risk to binge than those at the age of 13 and 14. The longer 15-year-old groups stay out with friends, the more likely are to take more drinks. There is also the chance that they would skip school days because of hangovers.

4.19   The risk of binge drinking on a night out

In question 11, students were asked to state how much they drink on a night out. The majority of 13-year-old boys reported that they usually drink between one to four drinks, whilst 60% 13-year-old girls reported that they normally drink from one to three drinks. About 40% 13-year-old girls reported that they drink a beer and vodka on a night out. About 92% 14-year-old boys have reported that they normally drink between three to twenty measures. There were about 7% 14-year-old boys who reported that they drink ten shooters and two vodkas on a night out and 1% reported usually drinks three beers and one bottle of wine on a night out.

About 68% 14-year old girls have reported that they usually drink between two to ten drinks, whilst about 32% of them have reported that they drink one bottle of wine, some shots of liquor, seven shooters and some cocktails on a night out. About 37% 15-year-old boys have reported that they usually drink between two to twenty glasses. There were about 53% 15-

year-old boys who reported drinking three to six beers and a two and a half bottles of wine on a night out, about 9% of them reported that they drink fourteen vodka and only 1% reported drinking thirty whiskies on a night out. There were about 85% 15-year-old girls who reported that they take between 0 to eight drinks. There were about 10% 15-year-old girls' participants who reported drinking two to five glasses of liquor, three glasses of wine and some beer and three vodkas. There were about 5% 15-year-old girls who reported that they drink until they get drunk. Table 4 below presents in brief what has been discussed.

Table 4

Binge drinking on a night out

GIRLS			BOYS		
60%	13 year old girls	1-3 drinks	100%	13 year old boys	1-4 drinks
40%	13 year old girls	1 Beer, 1 liquor	92%	14 year old boys	3-20 drinks
68%	14 year old girls	2-10 drinks	7%	14 year old boys	10 shooters, 2 liquors
32%	14 year old girls	1 bottle of wine, 1 glass liquor, 7 shooters, cocktails	1%	14 year old boys	3 beer, 1 bottle of wine
85%	15 year old girls	0-8 drinks	37%	15 year old boys	2-20 drinks
10%	15 year old girls	2-5 liquors, 3 glasses wine, some beer, 3 vodkas	53%	15 year old boys	6 beers, 2 ½ bottles of wine
5%	15 year old girls	Drink until they get drunk	9%	15 year old boys	14 liquors
			1%	15 year old boys	30 whiskeys

From this analysis, one may conclude that girls drink more alcohol on a night out compared with the boys. However, a comparison is made here. Whilst in section 4.4, results have demonstrated that males tend to start drinking at an earlier age and to indulge in more excessive drinking than females, in this section, girls drink more alcohol than boys.

This could be interpreted that girls are more socialized than boys and that boys drink to experiment with alcohol and to show off with friends.

One may comment that the figures in the table seem to be a bit exaggerated. One could also take into consideration that if young people are telling the truth, alcohol in clubs and pubs may either be providing a reduced volume of alcohol or alcohol is diluted in its strength with another non-alcoholic liquid.

4.20 Paceville as a venue of entertainment

Paceville is an area with the largest concentration of nightclubs, restaurants, multi-complex cinemas, coffee shops, and shopping centres. It is less than quarter of a square mile and has grown rapidly into an entertainment centre, where it is frequented by many young people from all over the island.

An interesting part for the students was (question 13) when they were asked to mention the clubs in Paceville, which they think, are the most popular amongst young people. The researcher required this information to find out which places in Paceville are subject to underage drinking, so as to see whether responses in the questionnaires were truthful or not. It is interesting to note that students between 13 and 15 years old know the types of places in Paceville, which are very popular amongst young people; therefore, these young people have been let into the nightclubs illegally.

Are there any other places available for young people to entertain themselves instead of Paceville? There were students who stated that there are not enough places of entertainment. As a result, young people have no alternative but to entertain themselves in Paceville, even if the area is considered an adult venue.

The following were the comments of young people concerning the atmosphere in Paceville. There were students who do not go to Paceville, but still think it is an interesting place and that it makes sense. Many students describe Paceville as a place of excitement, entertaining, energetic and enjoyable, a place to drink and dance, a place where everyone can have fun. They also described Paceville as a place of socializing, a place to unwind and a place to relax and feel comfortable, cool, funky and modern.

Others describe Paceville as hyperactive for young people, very noisy at night, very crowded and freaky, also been described as very bad, boring and even scary. Paceville also seems to be a place that does not make sense, very stupid, crazy and mad and always the same. They reported that there would be many rude, annoying and drunken people. A 14-year-old student commented: 'I like it because you are free to do anything'. Some 14-year-old students have also reported they saw even people taking drugs. Does this mean that in Paceville everyone can do whatever he/she wants, even if it is criminal and/or antisocial?

Photo 1

Partial view of Paceville early in the morning

Photo 2

Partial views of Paceville late at night

4.21 ID cards requested in Paceville

In Malta, every person has to have an Identity Card (ID) including young people at the age of 14 and over. At the age of 14, an ID card is issued, valid for two years. At 16, another ID card is issued for those at the age of sixteen, valid also for two years. The adult ID card is issued at the age of 18 and is valid for 5 years. After 5 years, another ID card will be provided.

The ID card contains the photo of the individual, the card number, the address, the individual's signature and the signature of the Police Commissioner. On the back of the ID card there is the date of birth on the individual, the valid dates of issue and expiry and the sequence number, the birth place, the nationality and sex. Details of the person's identity are in Maltese and English. Samples of ID cards are shown below. For ethical purposes, the persons' identity and the details contained herewith are blurred and unrecognized.

Figure 3

The Identity (ID) Cards

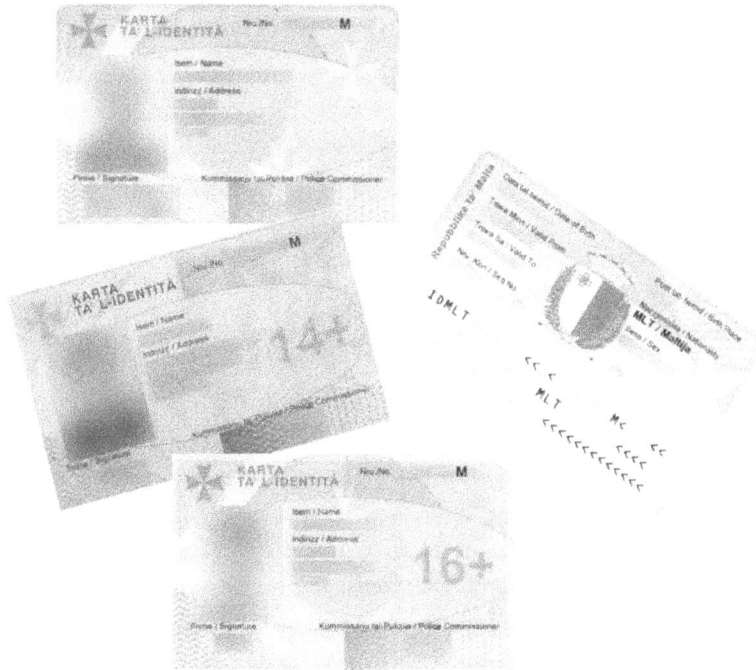

It was the researcher's intention to see whether door supervisors ask for IDs when young people go to clubs or bars in Paceville. A door supervisor has been defined by the Home Office as 'a person employed on premises which have a music and dancing license [Public Entertainment License – PEL] in operation with authority from the owner or landlord, exclusively or mainly, to decide upon the suitability of customers to be allowed on these premises; and/or to maintain order on those premises' (Home Office, 1995).

Students (48%) have reported that there is a high percentage of door supervisors' requesting for ID cards (Figure 4). 24% reported that door supervisors do not ask for ID cards whilst there were 28% who reported that only sometimes door supervisors ask for ID cards.

Figure 4

Door supervisors request for ID cards in Paceville

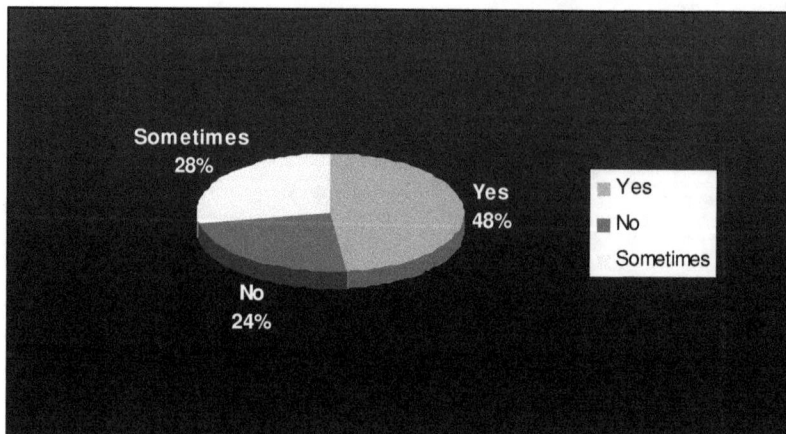

4.22 Problems with ID cards

Generally, girls had fewer problems with ID than boys, but all see it as simply an irritation to be overcome where necessary and obtaining false ID was reported to be easy. A fifteen-year-old girl reported 'I went into a club and the security asked me for ID. I said I did not have it with me and told him that I was sixteen and believed me'. Even where venues did not allow entry, simply obtaining alcohol was not seen as a problem. Respondents had a variety of strategies from getting to know a retailer, to asking strangers or older siblings to buy alcohol on their behalf.

4.23 The person who does not frequent Paceville

A person who does not frequent Paceville or drink alcohol is described as a person who is normal, strong and reliable, quiet, healthy and keeps out of trouble. He/she is described as a person who really cares about school and knows how to enjoy life. A fourteen-year-old group described that person as genuine and sensible, mature, cool and knows how to have fun. He/she is open minded, courageous, very responsible, certainly clean and wise. Others described that person as a nerd, a baby and immature, does not know how to enjoy life, does not afford to go to Paceville and/or parents do not allow him/her.

4.24   Students' awareness on Maltese Legislation

Question 29 was set up to test students' awareness on the use of alcohol drinking among young people. It is illegal to sell alcohol to someone under the age of 16 in Malta and they should not be allowed inside a place of entertainment. The question was: 'Do you think that the Maltese Law prohibits youth at your age from drinking alcohol?' The results presented were as follows. 15% of thirteen-year-old boys and girls indicated that there is a Law that prohibits youths under the age of sixteen from drinking alcohol whilst 6% did not agree. 25% of fourteen-year-old students agree that there is a Law. On the contrary, 12% of fourteen-year-old boys and girls disagreed that there is a Law. Students from the fifteen-year-old group age indicated that a Law exists but 15% did not agree.

From this data, it is clear that students are not aware of the Maltese Legislation. They are not aware that there is no legislation that prohibits underage drinking. However, there is some sort of legislation (chapter 2), which only prohibits adults including retailers from selling or supplying alcohol to minors. Only 33% who disagreed were correct.

4.25   Students' perceptions on the enforcement of Laws on alcohol

The last question was set up to give the initiative to all participants to suggest what Laws they would adapt with regards to alcohol, if they were a Member of Parliament (MP). The following comments are contents, which have been reported carefully.

Thirteen-year-old adolescents think that alcohol drinking should be prohibited for young people below the age of fourteen, fifteen and sixteen. Police should arrest or fine people who are caught selling alcohol to minors. Fourteen-year-old boys and girls think that they would not let people get drunk and prohibit drinking in public. Fourteen-year-old students think they would prohibit young people from drinking alcohol until they are eighteen and/or twenty-one years of age and suggested that they would prohibit alcohol use to those who are under the age of eighteen. Students added that they would totally forbid alcohol to young people at bars and ensure that the police are at every doorstep of every club or bar to check this.

Moreover, there were students who said that they would not allow those who are under the age of 16 to go to Paceville, as Paceville leads to temptation. There were 14-year-old students who reported that they would not do anything about Laws on alcohol because the problem is that there are many people who are still disobeying the Law. So why bother? One of the students from Non-State schools reported that when he wanted to take drugs and alcohol, access to him was very easy.

Some young people believe that from thirteen to sixteen years old, the individual can drink alcohol as long as he/she drinks responsibly and to a certain limit. There were others who said that young people should be over the age of eighteen and must present their Identity Cards. Fifteen-year-old adolescents think that young people should be allowed to do whatever they like. Others believe that young people under the age of sixteen should be warned and after three warnings, then they should be fined. A 15 year-old student from a Non-State school provided a suggestion and commented that alcohol should be available for young people. However, he stated that 'they can drink beer over sixteen years of age, liquor over the age of eighteen and drinking should be prohibited for children under the age of fourteen'. There were others who suggested that those who sell alcohol to young people should be penalized and argued that young people should only drink with their parents' consent.

With regards to the security, young people believe that there should be strict security on those who drink more than three measures. 'In Paceville, retailers are still selling alcohol to young people even though they are not supposed to sell alcohol to minors. All they care about is money'. A fourteen-year-old student from a Non-State school has expressed this comment. In general, students believe that there should be harsher Laws, which discourage people selling alcohol to minors, increase security and increase taxes on alcohol. Students put forward other ideas, for example, people who are caught drinking and driving, should have their license removed for a period. Underage drinking and driving goes beyond the scope of this dissertation. This issue is subject to specific research and more debate.

SECTION II

4.26 Focus groups

The researcher led focus groups and discussions amongst the participants. There were 24 mixed participants, six students from each school, boys and girls, thirteen to fifteen year olds, who took part and shared their experiences with the researcher. Focus group sessions took between one to two hours each and all records were documented. The researcher did not impose any limits on the participants on what to say. Students were asked about their drinking behaviour and attitudes. They answered questions about how often they drink, where and what they drink, why they drink, how much they drink, with whom and what expectations and consequences they had experienced. These discussions encouraged consistency and sharing of ideas within the groups. This discussion represented a wide cross section in terms of students' background and the attitudes and opinions of drinking experiences and habits. The questions asked by the researcher appear in bold in this text. The comments will follow.

4.27 "What have you been taught about alcohol?"

About two thirds of thirteen-year-olds argued that alcohol damages the brain, so one needs to think of the consequences before drinking or getting drunk. Others commented that alcohol is a drug in itself and it can be fatal if people drink and drive. Virtually all thirteen year olds have argued that alcohol can lead to violence. There were others who reported that due to excessive alcohol consumption people might live a shorter life. They also reported that alcohol might become a habit and leads to addiction.

About one third of fourteen-year-olds reported that 'too much' alcohol for one person does not mean 'too much' for another. It depends on the threshold of a person's drinking habit. Students have also reported that underage drinking is illegal. Many did not know whether it is illegal to drink under sixteen or eighteen years of age. Fourteen year olds reported that alcohol is bad for the liver and that a person can become an alcoholic. 'Alcohol can lead to violence and if people do not realize this risk, it can become too late to stop the onset of violence'. This was one of the comments from a fourteen-year-old girl.

Fifteen-year-old adolescents think that drinking too much alcohol is dangerous. They believe that everyone can drink but in moderation. They reported that people can loose concentration when drinking alcohol and if it is mixed with drugs, it could be fatal.

Alcohol appeared to fit extremely positively with the needs and aspirations of young people - particularly to have fun and to be included in peer groups and activities. To a certain degree, it was also regarded as a solution to their problems, especially with regards to social interactions. Drinking alcohol generates fun, which appears to be very important in this discussion.

4.28 "Do boys and girls behave differently when they drink?"

Adolescents argued that young people react differently. Girls argued that boys act silly when they drink alcohol. They added that boys become aggressive and violent when they drink alcohol. However, boys do not have any sexual inhibitions. Boys said the opposite and that when girls drinking alcohol, they become easier to talk with, gain more confidence, laugh more and become more emotional.

4.29 "How much money do you spend on alcoholic drinks at weekends?"

Some fourteen-year-old students reported that they spend between Lm 5.00 (equiv. £ 9.00) and Lm 15.00 (equiv. £ 25.00). Fifteen-year-old students reported that they spend between Lm 3.00 (equiv. £ 6.00) to Lm 7.00 (equiv. £ 13.00) on alcohol per week.

4.30 Fears and Level of Security in Paceville

Students were requested to mention what would frighten them most in Paceville and give suggestions in order to make sure that Paceville is secure at all times. Thirteen year olds reported that they are afraid of fights, people of a different race and stalkers. Fourteen year olds reported the same adding rape and violence especially when door supervisors get involved. Fifteen year olds reported that they are afraid of harassment, crowds, stalkers, guns, knives and drugs.

Boys reported that there should be more police surveillance and more door supervisors in Paceville. However, one of the students commented: 'if police patrol the place, especially at weekends, the place will be ruined'. Girls gave negative comments and did not have much enthusiasm on improving the place. It seems that although Paceville is a venue of entertainment, fears exist in young people. What is surprising is that young people know that the place is not secure and they also have the perception that there is nothing much one can do. Even if there is, police presence is regarded alien and young people might feel that Paceville will be another prison. Therefore, the pleasure will diminish.

4.31   Stress, pressure and alcohol consumption on young people

Although not in the majority, there were a number of references to the use of alcohol for helping the individual to relax and cope with stress. In some cases, the source of stress was clearly identified: pressure of examinations or a family problem. Popular perceptions among young people about alcohol use among their peers would appear to support these findings. Initial responses to questions about peer pressure in focus groups normally met with assertions that individuals would be pressurised into drinking. The majority of males and females reported that sometimes it makes one feel awkward and embarrassed, if only friends are drinking. Subsequent discussions in focus groups led to many young people admitting that they felt pressured to drink the same amounts as their friends and companions.

4.32   Health and Safety

The last question, the researcher asked was about Health and Safety. Using taxis to get home safely was a common strategy, but taxis can be very expensive and it was acknowledged they might still have to walk home, increasing the risk, especially if they were alone. The researcher also encouraged students to say what they would do to get home safely after a night out with friends. Thirteen-year-old students said that they go home with parents. Many students said that they arrange lifts beforehand with parents or bus the trip back home with friends.

SECTION III

4.33 Observation methodology in Paceville

This brief analysis illustrates the method, results, and implications of some observational research in Paceville. The researcher's role was to focus on the physical and social environment in Paceville, assess the level of security in this place and the drinking patterns of young people. Hereunder, the researcher reports the exact details and events of what it has been observed.

4.33.1 Details and events reported

Observation sessions were conducted on Thursday 23, Friday 24 December 2004 and between Friday and Saturday 31 December 2004 / 1 January 2005. Nine visits lasting two hours each session were made during the periods of observation. Each club, on average, was visited twice. The observation periods were divided into three phases: early i.e. from 8pm to midnight, middle i.e. midnight to 2am and early in the morning i.e. from 2am to 5am. Therefore, when choosing the first phase, the researcher chose any two hours between 8 pm and midnight.

Paceville has poor parking facilities, poor lighting and there is a minimal police presence. There are no security cameras outside clubs and pubs; but there are spot cameras. These were probably installed because Paceville centre is a pedestrian area, however, cars can still pass through. One can expect incidents, even vandalism, in an environment where thousands of young people congregate to entertain themselves. Thus, for the great number of people that visit Paceville, there are few police and some of the incidents may go unnoticed.

Door supervisors seem to be racists. They are intolerant of a different religion and of different skin colour, thus these people are the first to be thrown out of the bar, even if they have done nothing wrong. In Paceville, there are cinemas, a bowling alley, and a shopping complex that remains open until late, having a number of facilities, such as a games room, many coffee and cake shops, restaurants and clothes shops.

There were girls and boys appearing to be under the age of 16 that went into the same pub at the same time all throughout the observation. On two incidents, the researcher clearly noticed a young male covering the identity of the photo in the card as shown in Figure 5, solely to reveal the number, as described in the questionnaire and in the pilot study. On another incident, the ID card of a young female was waved about, to act like a flashcard, which the door supervisor could not focus on.

Covering the owner's Identity

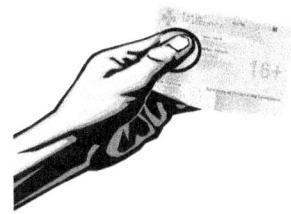

Figure 5

The door supervisor did not take notice, but paid attention to scantiness of clothing the girl was wearing. Young males tended to stay in their own groups, with their own friends. They were friendly and cheerful but male hostility and roughness, appeared to be from low to medium levels, with some swearing thrown in. Female young people tended to be in groups and more scattered their dresses revealing even scanty. Overall, there were low levels of female hostility, roughness, bumping and rowdiness but with similar swearing levels as with males.

The researcher identified three high-risk premises based on first-hand knowledge, the Bootleggers, Mosquito, and Pit Stop. Bootleggers, Mosquito and Pit Stop are mainly bars, with very little space to move around. These clubs are not comfortable, not attractive or clean. Toilets were left dirty at all times. Unattractive venues tended to be the least comfortable and poorly supervised, but were the most frequented by young people.

Crowding was a major problem in each of the club that was visited, even those apart from the above. In order to recognize the difference, the researcher went to other clubs, which were not mentioned by young people, these catered for people of about 20. The atmosphere was not much different, except for the club being larger and more pleasant.

Thousands of people from the different strata of Maltese society are packed into a relatively small area. From the observation, it seems that younger people have no problem buying alcohol. Plenty of alcohol is available and this sometimes leads to trouble and violence. The researcher observed some violent acts in Paceville during the early hours of the morning and the majority being stopped by the circle of friends, not by security. There were four verbal aggression incidents observed, which were not severe. There was only one incident where the ambulance had to be called for a 23-year-old male, sitting down on the kerb with a friend next to him, who was forced out of the club with a nasty punch in the face.

The young people involved in aggressive behaviour were told to leave the premises immediately, usually by the barmen who attended the club rather than by the security. Only one incident of property damage was recorded, the police were immediately informed. During a fight, bottles were meant to be thrown at two people but accidentally hit a closed glass door, again during the early hours of the morning. The researcher tried to go unnoticed and moved away whenever a fight or an unpleasant social event occurred.

On two occasions the security were stopping people from leaving clubs with a bottle of drink in their hands. People say that in Paceville, one will be fined for carrying a bottle out of a disco, club, or pub. This however was not implemented and there were no notices or signs inside or outside clubs. There were occasions where people carried bottles of beer for their friends who were talking outside. If the security stopped them, they would talk him out of it and promise not to do it again. Apart from older people, the drinks that the young people took outside consisted mainly of beer, coke bottles, and Red Bull.

The venues of entertainment visited during the observation provided adequate numbers of bartenders, who were generally male staff. Female staff was present for entertainment, but had a share behind the bar when one of the male bartenders was not present. Shooters (mixed cocktail) were the most common drink consumed amongst young people, as also stated in the pilot study.

On every occasion during the observation, there were special offers on drinks, encouraging people to drink, for example, a double vodka drink for a little higher price than a single vodka drink. These offers were different from one club to another; however, drinks were bought quite frequently because of the offer. On Christmas and New Years Eve, the prices of the drinks were again reduced, introducing 'buy one get one free', again encouraging people to drink heavily. Apart from adults, young people were also involved and bought drinks according to the special offers.

In one particular club, the largest one out of the three mentioned, young people were challenging each other to drink and then walk straight. The one who keeps upright would be challenged again to keep drinking. Young people were therefore challenging each other to keep drinking until they get drunk. The majority of drinks were consumed from either bottles or cans. Female drunkenness was slightly lower than that of males.

According to the researcher's observation, door supervisors in Paceville seem poorly trained, obsessed with their own bodybuilding image which does not reduce trouble but may rather agree with a hostile and aggressive atmosphere. In practice, many door supervisors are not well trained in their work and appear to be given a job autonomy and discretion that they cannot handle well.

It is far easier and surely consistent with broad considerations of the public good, to regulate routine activities of the venues in Paceville frequently. The best way of doing this is to restrict the activities of the worst 'hot spots' by licence cancellation. Other reforms in regulatory practices may have the potential to improve greatly the safety of Paceville for thousands of young people who rely on this place to be the most attractive place of entertainment.

4.34 Summary of the analysis, results and conclusion

Underage drinking in Malta is a problem. 86% of students under the age of 16 have reported alcohol consumption in their lifetime. This is because of excessive pressure from school, parents, peers, and/or other social reasons. The data represented in this chapter indicates that the majority of respondents have been drinking alcohol from the age of 10 and that 3% of this sample has already experienced drunkenness at the age of 10 years. 38% boys and 47% girls say that they would be drinking alcohol when they are 25.

From these analyses, one may deduce that there is a high percentage of those who drink alcohol because they want to feel good (36%) followed by knowing that it is harmful but they do not care (17%) and want to forget their problems (16%). The data indicates that there are a high percentage of 15-year-old boys (28%) and 15-year-old girls (17%) who reported that adults bought alcohol for them during the last three years. A number of students have reported that they usually drink with their family. Nevertheless, girls and boys enter pubs and clubs at a young age and are given drinks. The analyses revealed that young people consume alcohol mostly from discos and nightclubs.

Students are not aware that no legislation exists to prohibit alcohol use amongst young people under the legal drinking age. Although there is a Law that forbids selling alcohol drinks to minors and persons under sixteen are not be allowed inside a place of entertainment, the Law however is neither being supported by the community not strictly enforced. Young people resort to drinking and retailers ascertain themselves by flaunting the Law.

About 48% of the students reported that the door supervisors were requesting ID cards prior entering a club in Paceville. The researcher, however, saw that the majority of door supervisors (all males), avoided asking young girls for ID cards at the doors. Many young people remain in Paceville until dawn, especially if these young people go out on Saturday – literally their night out.

In this chapter, the results obtained from the study were presented and the main objectives of the study have been positively reached. The following chapter will present the discussion, recommendations, and conclusions of the study.

Discussion, Recommendations & Conclusion

DISCUSSION: Introduction

Prevention of underage drinking mainly has two goals. The first goal is to prevent harm to the individual drinker and the second is to prevent harm to the society. Prevention strategies can be measured by their results, which include reducing the number of antisocial events, reducing the amount of harm to individuals and reducing criminal and juvenile justice costs. One also has to consider medical and other treatment expenses.

Malta has not yet become conscious of this problem and this lack of awareness cannot be kept outside the microcosm of society. As schools are an integrated part of society, they cannot be presumed immune to the ways of the world. Identifying the risk factors of underage drinking in its earlier stages may be the most efficient way to combat abuse. It is our mission therefore, to protect minors from alcohol abuse and provide security to our children.

Security as defined by Scarman (2001a: (1) 1-16) is 'a condition of safety, freedom from danger particularly freedom from the risk of criminal victimization, worries or anxieties. 'Security provides those means, active or passive, which serve to protect and preserve an environment that allows for the conduct of activities within the organization or society without disruption.'

The recommendations proposed in this chapter are for the perusal of the Maltese Government, National, and local non-profit agencies, professional associations and for the public. There is no simple solution; the recommendations proposed have been made upon careful analysis.

RECOMMENDATIONS

5.1   Sedqa and Caritas as Learning Organizations

Recommendation 1 - Sedqa and Caritas should assess the underage drinking problem and consider effective approaches such as community organizing and the strategic use of the mass media to reduce drinking among underage young people. Sedqa and Caritas should not only target people with the problem, but their approach to the problem. This means that instead of preaching and making young people bored or possibly confuses young people's minds; they should be organisations with an ingrained philosophy for anticipating, reacting, and responding to change, complexity, and uncertainty. Instead of stigmatizing alcohol and trying to scare people into abstinence, it is better to demonstrate the hazardous effects that alcohol might have on the alcoholic individual. It is important for young people to recognize that it is not alcohol itself but rather the abuse of alcohol that is the problem. There is also little point in knowing how to prevent alcohol abuse if no action steps are taken to reduce the problem. Alcohol abuse should be regarded as a different aspect of substance abuse and given due importance.

It is therefore the duty of these learning organisations to give:

- Information on civil and criminal liability when supplying alcohol to young people.
- Quality information describing the signs and symptoms of a child abusing alcohol.
- Proper education on risk and protective factors associated with alcohol use; and
- Parenting skills directed at youth alcohol use.

5.2 Identifying the risk factors for alcohol misuse

Recommendation 2 - The risk factors for alcohol misuse can be categorised into three groups namely family, school and community strategies.

i. Family strategies

Family strategies for preventing alcohol misuse and abuse should incorporate structured, home-based parent-child activities, family skills training, behavioural parent training, and behavioural family therapy.

Parents must improve their relations by using positive reinforcement with their children, enhance listening and communication skills, and help on problem solutions. Parents must educate their children about the dangers of alcohol and early alcohol use. Most importantly, parents should be educated not to allow their children taste alcohol at a very young age. As demonstrated in all questionnaires, none of the young people disagreed that alcohol tastes horrible. In the Maltese society, parents are not aware of the socializing of their children and are almost not aware of their drinking habits. In this respect, Sedqa and Caritas can also contribute by organizing special training to educate parents as to how the messages they give to their children regarding alcohol are grasped by their children.

ii.   School strategies

Strategies to modify school-based risk factors would incorporate personal, social and resistance skills, interactive teaching techniques, teacher training and support, active family and community involvement. Schoolteachers should continuously enhance the skills young people need to cope with negative environmental and peer pressure including resistance, refusal and assertiveness skills. In this respect, a Personal and Social Development Programme (PSD) is essential not only throughout the secondary school years but also in the higher classes of primary school. The aim of the PSD programmes should be to empower individuals as they develop personal attributes such as self-esteem, assertiveness, social skills, and group skills.

The PSD programmes should be interesting and not boring for young people, who might have a tendency to ignore the lessons once the subject does not apply to them. Something that might also be interesting for young people is to hear other people's thoughts and experiences on the subject in question, in this case alcohol. This would involve obtaining consent from an ex-alcoholic, who might be willing to talk his or her personal experience. Combined with the medical aspect and the effects that alcohol might have on the body, the speaker may be able to get the message across to young people. This may be as a sort of lesson 'true-to-life', that is, a person that has passed from the experience, shares his/her views with other people, to encourage them not to fall into the same trap. These lessons may also be for other subjects that might be of interest to young people, for example, drugs, sex at a very young age and its responsibilities, discussion of a different religion, time management, improvement of familial and friend relationships and voluntary work. Many subjects are interesting and all have the interesting points, which the young adolescent may use further on in life.

iii.   Community strategies

The risk factors of community vulnerabilities are caused by the easy availability of alcohol and community disorganisation. Strategies to reduce underage drinking should include the involvement of the media to increase alcohol awareness. Given the extensive nature of alcohol abuse in our society, apart from Sedqa and Caritas, this issue should be addressed within the context of mainstream disciplines and occupations such as Education, Medicine, Nursing, Psychology, Public Health, Criminology, Law, Security, Social Work, Occupational Therapy, and allied professionals. The entire community should therefore be behind a message that everyone would support an alcohol-free lifestyle for young people.

5.3   Educational Campaigns

Recommendation 3 - Educational campaigns need to be accompanied by new Legislation that empowers the police to enforce the Law. Since 2001, The Sense Group promoted a very clear message against alcohol misuse. The Sense Group are a group of parents that support Sedqa and Caritas's views against the distribution of alcohol to young people. They promoted this campaign on radio, newspapers, and cinemas. If similar campaigns had to be implemented, they would raise awareness on alcohol problems supported by effective policies linked with proven intervention. Mr Joe Farrugia, the chief Executive Officer of The Sense Group stated that '…Here we have a clear example which shows what can be achieved when the authorities, the social aspects organisations and the public work together' (The Malta Business Weekly, 2001).

5.4   The media in Malta on alcohol advertisement

Recommendation 4 - In Malta effective underage anti-drinking messages need to be severely developed and current messages need to be expanded in hopes of reaching young people that may be experimenting in alcohol use very early in their lives. Usually, the only advertisements that one may see are general advertisements in the local newspapers, mentioning the 'do's and don'ts' of drinking, rather than underage drinking.

Where the media is concerned, the Public Broadcasting Authority (PBA) in Malta on 9 February 2001 has published guidelines on alcoholic drink advertising to be read in conjunction with paragraph 19 of the Third Schedule to the Broadcasting Act (Cap.350 of the Laws of Malta). These guidelines are found on World Wide Web and are shown in Appendix L.

5.5   Alcohol and Juvenile Delinquency

As far as Malta is concerned, the Juvenile Court Act provides for the setting up of an 'ad hoc' court to deal with young persons under the age of 16 years, who act in a deviant manner. This means that minors under the age of 9 years are exempt from criminal responsibility (s.35, Cap. 9). This applies also for the young persons under the age of 14 years behaving mischievously. Another part of legislation - the Children and Young Persons (Care Orders) Act (Cap. 285), provides the necessary measures for placing a child under the care of the Minister for social welfare (Ferola, 2002).

Although not all young people who binge are likely to be Lawbreakers, there is the possibility that most of young people who binge may become a social threat to the society. The goal is to stop delinquency before it begins. Delinquency can more often measured using youth self-reports than official records of arrest or conviction in evaluations of school-based prevention programs.

In a small country such as Malta where everybody knows one another, teachers and other educators are a useful resource and can identify children who may become tomorrow's delinquents. Any person concerned for the wellbeing of the child, society should be encouraged to provide the resources and the necessary structures required to set up these intervention programmes.

In 1925, Cyril Burt laid out the following 'manifesto' of social crime prevention, in which the influence of positivism is easy to see:

1.   'All young persons who show delinquent tendencies should be dealt with at the earliest possible stage. Parents should be taught that the pre-school is a period vitally decisive...Teachers should be urged to watch, and where necessary to report, all who show antisocial inclinations...When the school period is over, after care workers should be persuaded to extend their supervision to the social conduct, as well as the industrial efficiency, of children who have just left, and, above all, special efforts should be made to meet the transitional phase of adolescence'(Burt, 1925).

2.   'The problem of delinquency in young must be envisaged as but one inspirable portion of the larger enterprise for child welfare. Crime in children is not a unique, well marked, or self-contained phenomenon, to be handled solely by the policeman or the children's court. It touches every side of social work. The teacher, the care committee worker, the magistrate, the probation officer, all who come into official contact with the child, should be working hand in hand not only with each other, but with all the clubs, societies and agencies, voluntary as well as public, that seek to better the day-to-day life of the child' (Burt, 1925).

3.   'The delinquent himself must be approached individually as a unique human being with a peculiar constitution, peculiar difficulties, and peculiar problems of his own...The court, therefore, and whatever authority has to grapple with such cases must all times regard not the offence, but the offender. The aim must not be punishment, but treatment; and the target not isolated actions, but their causes...Such authorities must have access to all available information and possess means to make for every case intensive investigations of their own...A social investigator must report on home circumstances; a medical officer must inspect the child for physical defects; a psychologist must be at hand to apply mental tests, to assess temperamental qualities, and to analyse unconscious motives. A psychological clinic embodying all these different workers studying the same causes scientifically, side by side, is the most pressing need of all' (Burt, 1925).

4.   'The remedies, in the same way, will be adapted, not to the nature of the offence, but to the nature of the factors provoking it. Probation should be employed with a larger freedom and at the same time with finer discrimination; it should include, for each separate case, not merely passive surveillance, but active and constructive efforts... After-care, in particular, calls for further extension; to lavish a hundred pounds upon the intensive training of a youth in an institution and then suddenly letting him loose into the old environment, sparing neither time nor trouble for further aid or following-up, is not economy but waste' (Burt, 1925).

5.   'Fuller knowledge is urgently wanted: it is wanted both in regard to the causation of crime and in respect of the relative efficacy of different remedial measures. Only from the organisation of research can this fuller knowledge come, and organised research means an established criminological department. The fruits of some research should be made immediately accessible to the practical officer, and courses of instruction should be arranged where all who have to deal with the young offender may learn the latest and best accredited results of modern psychology' (Burt, 1925).

6.   'Finally, society must aim at prevention as well as at cure. Housing, medical treatment, continued education, the psychological study of children in schools, improved industrial conditions, increased facilities for recreation, the cautious adoption of practical eugenic measures, and above all, sustained investigation into all the problems of childhood – these are but a few of the countless needs to be supplied, if delinquency in the young is to be not merely cured as it arises, but diverted, forestalled, and so far as possible wiped out' (Burt, 1925).

(Burt, 1925:584-97, quoted in Scarman Centre 2001 (1): 6-10 – 6-12)

5.6   Treatment of alcohol abuse

Recommendation 5 - The Government of Malta should provide enough financial assistance for the treatment of youths and their families who are facing alcohol related problems. The government should also provide training to pediatricians, medical experts and other health service providers on screening for signs of alcohol abuse and expand treatment services to children with special needs.

5.7   Entertainment facilities

Luzin and Orem (1967) saw beneficial effects in recreation provision they found that:

1) Recreation can lure the potential delinquent away from criminal activities without the use of sanction.

2) It provides a medium in which behaviour can be examined and problems identified.

3) It can develop rapport between youth and youth leaders, which can form a basis of successful delinquency prevention.

4) Recreation is a therapy for emotional problems.

However, as seen from the questionnaires, young people have argued that in Malta, there is no where to go apart from the only place of entertainment which is Paceville.

A comprehensive literature review (Scales and Leffert, 1999) on the effects of involvement in youth programs such as sports, recreation, camps, mentoring and drop-in centers on adolescent development, is associated with better development of life skills, greater communication skills, fewer psychosocial problems, decreased involvement in risky behaviors, such as alcohol misuse, decreased juvenile delinquency and violence and decreased risk of dropping out of school. Therefore the opening of small entertainment facilities with the provisional sale of cocktails made from juices and non-alcoholic drinks made be sufficient for young people to entertain themselves without spoiling the event by getting drunk or bingeing.

Recommendation 6 - Providing leisure facilities, particularly for actual and potential juvenile delinquents, may reduce offences, as recreation can enhance the young person's self-esteem. Cinemas, youth clubs, and community centres are all alternative strategies for effective prevention measures. The Government of Malta should therefore cooperate with the beneficiaries and the public to provide a special funding for everyone that can afford to pool in money for more drama schools, sport complexes and other entertainment places.

5.8   Official statistics on underage drinking offences

Recommendation 7 - Consideration needs to be given to the feasibility of collecting official statistics routinely at a national level, which will provide a true picture of the impact of alcohol on crime. The main obstacle faced by the researchers in Malta is that no official statistics are available on alcohol related crime. Underage drinking offences are not currently notifiable to the Police or the National Office of Statistics.

5.9   Enforcing underage drinking Laws in Malta

Recommendation 8 - It is recommended that the legal drinking age in Malta is raised from 16 to 21. This recommendation is based on the study of Grant, et al (1997) as discussed in chapter 2, who stated that if drinking is delayed until age 21, a child's risk of serious alcohol related problems would be decreased by 70%.

These initiatives should include the enforcement of Minimum Purchase Age Laws (MPAL), the possession and consumption of alcohol by minors and sales of alcohol to minors. Although the minimum drinking age Laws in Malta prohibit purchase or attempted purchase, possession and consumption of alcoholic beverages by persons under 16, such Legislations should also prohibit possession of and use of falsified or fraudulent identification to purchase or attempt to purchase alcoholic beverages and provision of any alcohol to minors by adults, except to their own children in their own residences.

According to the researcher's observation, Malta has many shops, clubs, pubs, and discothèques who sell alcohol to young people. Maltese authorities should enforce the Law related to providing alcohol for minors. Licensees should be held responsible for behaviour of underage young people as well as for the illegal sale of alcohol.

5.10 Wardens Role Extension

Recommendation 9 – The Maltese Wardens should extend their role by working with the police to reduce underage drinking in public locations, such as beaches, parking lots, recreation facilities and at village *festi*. Wardens are therefore encouraged to act as capable guardians to reduce underage drinking and antisocial behaviour of young people in respect of alcohol misuse.

5.11 The Role of the Police Officers on underage drinking

Recommendation 10 - Police officers must be trained in conflict prevention, resolution and increased deployment of trained officers in a proactive role in Paceville particularly on the days mostly frequented by young people, usually at weekends and holidays. The police must also routinely cite underage drinkers and adults who supply alcohol to minors and perform breathalyser tests especially in Paceville.

5.12 The use of (Electronic) Identity Cards in Malta

Recommendation 11 - Police officers should enter an "on-premise" establishment and check the IDs of everyone drinking alcohol and watch out for fraudulent IDs. These ID checks encourage door supervisors to be careful in their efforts to verify customer age and show customers that the police support the establishment's policies and procedure.

Preventing underage drinking is a very complicated matter. In some European countries like Italy and Malta, ID cards are mandatory and can be used as proof of age. There are many who feel that an ID card system is an invasion of privacy, though, for the purposes of legal drinking ages, there should be some sort of identification scheme also operated in pubs and clubs.

Properly trained door supervisors in Paceville and electronic card systems may be able to detect false IDs and more likely to refuse to let in young people in discos, bars or pubs. The use of electronic ID cards may also apply to those who normally sell alcohol from shops. It is up to the Government and voluntary organizations to ensure or at least try to encourage shop owners to be more co-operative in this venture.

5.13 Age Verification Device

Figure 6

Recommendation 12 - One way to limit youth access to alcohol is to enforce age 16 Laws more harshly at the retail level. When used properly and consistently, age verification devices (Figure 6) take the burden of proof off the retailer and place it on the individuals who may be attempting to purchase alcohol. These devices are known as the age/identity verification technology, electronic age verification devices, magnetic stripe license technology, and magnetic card or stripe readers, are simple and easy to use.

The ID is swiped in as if a bank's money card and the ID number appears on the screen. Some machines provide a readable prompt on the display that clearly states, 'Underage Customer'. The apparatus as shown in the diagram and the information about the age verification device is found on World Wide Web.

5.14 The introduction of (CCTVs) cameras in Paceville

Recommendation 13 - The introduction of closed circuit television (CCTV) systems is one of the best methods to be used in a wide variety of applications. It can detect and monitor criminal activity such as drinking disorder in a wide variety of applications.

'The truth is that CCTV is a powerful tool that society is only just beginning to understand. It looks simple to use, but it is not. It has many components and they can impact in different ways. It is more than just a technical solution; it requires human intervention to work to maximum efficiency and the problems it helps deal with are complex. There needs to be greater recognition that reducing and preventing crime is not easy and that ill-conceived solutions are unlikely to work no matter what the investment' (Leicester University, 2005).

The value of the CCTVs however may enable police officers to 'see' potential problems on underage drinking or gangs of youths gathering and move them on before incidents. A better and capable equipped security or police will respond immediately to incidents or offences because of the notice they are given by the camera surveillance.

Security guards should be with constant radio contact and the patrolling guard should be given instructions to act if there is any particular situation that needs investigation. Should there be the slightest indication that a situation is getting out of hand; the police should immediately be called out. The patrolling officer should be equipped with a pager which will be used as a panic button connected to the police should the need arise. There should also be a record of the filming done by the CCTV cameras and retained for seven days unless such recording is being used to investigate a particular occurrence.

5.15 Training for Door Supervisors

Recommendation 14 - There is a major need to establish clear guidelines for the role and activity of door supervisors' staff in Paceville and other venues of entertainment. According to the researcher's observation, there are a number of clubs, which seem not to be skillfully managed and controlled. The researcher recommends standards of selection and training for door and security staff. Appropriate training should be a precondition for employing a person in the specific role of door supervisor. Such training should include Communication Skills, Procedures about Security duties and Functions, Security Measures, Licensing Law, Criminal

Law, Illegal Substance Abuse, First Aid, Fire Safety, Health and Safety, Customer Care, Quality Service and Conflict Management.

CONCLUSION

'Risk, Perception, awareness and preventive measures to reduce underage drinking and the illegal purchase of alcohol in Malta'. This was the subject of this dissertation under discussion, which focused on the social context of underage drinking in terms of crime, mental disorder, and social disability. This study aimed to reach its objectives by examining the problem of underage alcohol use in Malta among young people between the age of 13 and 15 years old and on the prevention strategies aimed to reduce this problem, which have been discussed and presented in this chapter. Studies of this nature would have been impossible without presenting the literature review as it built slowly and steadily on the work of past researchers; although it was very difficult for the researcher to gather Maltese Literature. This is because such data in Malta is limited or not available.

The review of the related literature and research was vital for the researcher and for the reader to grasp the knowledge and understanding on the subject being studied and the methods, which have been demonstrated. It was found out from the literature review that if a person abuses alcohol, he or she might become dependent upon alcohol and that the younger a person begins to drink, the greater the chance he or she will develop a problem with alcohol later in life.

The literature review has also presented the importance, nature and extent of underage alcohol use in Malta because it seems that this issue has been somehow forgotten. It was the researcher's intention to educate people in Malta about the use and misuse of youth drinking and put people on guard that the problem exists and that we seriously need to do something about it.

The researcher has hypothesised that underage drinking in Malta is a problem due to excessive pressure from school, parents, peers and/or other social reasons to an extent that they misuse alcohol and put their health and health of others at risk. Besides it was drawn that the Law is neither being supported by the community nor strictly enforced, particularly at venues of entertainment where young people resort to drinking and retailers ascertain themselves by flaunting the Law.

It was important for the researcher to test the hypothesis by knowing what young people think and feel about alcohol drinking, from where young people consume alcohol beverages and what prevention measures the authorities may take into perspective to reduce underage drinking and the illegal purchase of alcohol in Malta, particularly at venues of entertainment.

The researcher has considered the recipe of good research, which is made up of adequate data gathering techniques, the careful design, and piloting of measurement instruments or strategies and the systematic collection of data. The techniques, which have been used in the study, were the use of questionnaires, focus group discussions, and observational methods. Ethical considerations such as anonymity and confidentiality were also taken in to account.

The hypotheses were tested during the study and it was revealed that underage drinking in Malta is a problem as many students have reported a high consumption of alcohol at an early age. Young people in Malta drink to feel good and because they want to forget their problems. The majority of students reported that the usually drink with their family.

From the study, it was revealed that young people in Malta have misconception about Laws on alcohol. They are allowed to go to Paceville, enter pubs and clubs at a very young age, and be given drinks by retailers. It was revealed that many young people in Malta remain in Paceville until dawn and that Paceville is the only entertainment venue where young people in Malta spend their nightlife to enjoy and binge.

To be able to rest assure parents and young people's families, prevention measures were introduced in this dissertation for the purpose of everyone in Malta especially for our young people. These measures do not guarantee that underage drinking and the illegal sale of alcohol will diminish from our society, but the strategies employed have been illustrated in a way to reduce many problems in Malta on the abuse and misuse of alcohol if security measures had to be employed and the Law in Malta is to be enforced.

BIBLIOGRAPHY

Alcoholics Anonymous (2004) *Alcoholics Anonymous*
Continental European Region, http://www.aa-europe.net/, 18th June, 2004.

Anderson, E., and Quast, W. (1983) 'Young children in alcoholic families: A mental health needs-assessment intervention/prevention strategy', *Journal of Primary Prevention* 3:(3) 174-187.

Bailey, S. L., Pollock, N. K., Martin, C. S., and Lynch, K. G. (1999) *The National Center on Addiction and Substance Abuse (CASA),* Columbia University.

Barnes, J.A. (1979) 'Who Should Know What? Social Science, Privacy and Ethics', in N.Gilbert, (2001) Researching Social Life (eds) *Researching Social Life,* London: Sage Publications Ltd.

Barnhart, C.L., and Barnhart, R.K. (1992a) The World Book Dictionary (5th edn), Chicago: World Book, Inc, 10.

Barnhart C.L., and Barnhart, R.K., (1992b) The World Book Dictionary (5th edn), Chicago: World Book, Inc, 1331.

Bezzina, C., Clark, M., and Borg, M. (1997) *ESPAD: student survey in secondary schools, Malta, 1995,* Malta: Sedqa.

Broadcasting Authority, Malta (2001) *Guidelines on Alcoholic Drink Advertising,* http://www.ba-malta.org.mt/guidelines/m_code_alch_adv.htm, 22nd April, 2004.

Brown, S.A., Tapert, S.F., Granholm, E., and Delis, D.C. (2000) 'Neurocognitive functioning of adolescents: effects of protracted alcohol use', in International Center for Alcohol Policies 2004, *What drives underage drinking? An International Analysis,* Washington, DC.

Bulmer, M. (1982) 'The ethics of social research' in N. Gilbert (eds), *Researching Social Life,* London: Sage Publications Ltd.

Burt, C. (1925) *The Young Delinquent,* New York: Appleton in Scarman Centre (2001) *MSc in Security and Risk Management, Module 1,* Leicester: Scarman Centre, 6-10 – 6-12.

Caritas Malta (2004) *Caritas Malta on the side of people in need, http://www.caritasmalta.org/,* 18th June, 2004.

Central Office of Statistics (1998) Census of population and housing Malta, Volume 5: Migration, returned emigrants and miscellaneous, Malta: Author.

Cotton, N.S. (1979) 'The familial incidence of alcoholism: A review', *Journal of Studies on Alcohol,* 40:89-116.

Dawson, D.A. (2000) 'The link between family history and early onset alcoholism: Earlier initiation of drinking or more rapid development of dependence?' *Journal of Studies on Alcoholism,* 61(5): 637–646.

Deehan, A. (1999) 'Alcohol, the criminal justice system, the licensed industry and crime: A review of the current literature', in T. Honess, L. Seymour and R. Webster (eds), *The Social Contexts of underage drinking,* London: Crown.

Department of Health (1995) *Sensible Drinking: the report of an inter-departmental working group,* London: HMSO.

Department of Information (2004a) 'Young criminals, young victims', in The Sunday Times, March 24, 2002, http://www.doi.gov.mt/EN/commentaries/2003/04/ind27.asp, 14th July, 2004.

Department of Information (2004b) 'Drink control', in The Times, August 15, 2001, http://www.doi.gov.mt/EN/commentaries/2003/04/ind27.asp, 14th July, 2004.

DePoy E., and Gitlin L.N. (1998), *Introduction Research, Understanding and Applying Multiple Strategies, Data Gathering Strategies*, USA: Mosby Year Book Inc, 219-221.

Doweiko, H.E., (1990) *Concepts of Chemical Dependency*, Belmont CA: Brooks Cole Publishing.

Fergusson, D.M., Horwood, L.J. and Lynskey, M.T. (1995) 'The prevalence and risk factors associated with abusive or hazardous alcohol consumption in 16-year-olds', *Addiction*, 90: 935–46.

Fergusson, D.M., Lynskey, M.T. and Horwood, L.J. (1996a) 'Alcohol misuse and juvenile offending in adolescence', in T. Honess, L. Seymour and R. Webster (eds), *The Social Contexts of underage drinking,* London: Crown.

Fergusson, D.M., and Lynskey, M.T. (1996b) 'Alcohol misuse and adolescent sexual behaviours and risk taking', in International Center for Alcohol Policies 2004, *What drives underage drinking? An International Analysis,* Washington, DC.

Ferola, L. (2002) *Juvenile crime in the Applicant Countries: trends and prevention policies,* Fondazione Censis, http://www.censis.it/censis/jump/doc/en/index_3_a.html, 28th February, 2005.

Fletcher, L.A., Toomey, T.L., Wagenaar, A.C., Short, B., and Willenbring, M.L. (2000) 'Alcohol home delivery services: A source of alcohol for underage drinkers', *Journal of Studies on Alcohol,* 61(1), 81-84.

Flick, U. (1998) *An Introduction to Qualitative Research,* London: Sage, 116.

Fink, A. (1995) *The Survey Handbook: The Survey Kit 1, Thousand Oaks*, CA: Sage.

Gill, M. (1996) 'Risk, Security & Crime prevention: An International Forum for Developing Theory & Practice', International Journal of Risk, Security & Crime Prevention, 1 (1): 16.

Grant, B.F, Dawson D.A. (1997) 'Age at onset of alcohol use and association with DSM-IV alcohol abuse and dependence: Results from the National Longitudinal Alcohol Epidemiologic Survey', in International Center for Alcohol Policies 2004, *What drives underage drinking? An International Analysis,* Washington, DC.

Grech H. (2004) *Maltese Boys drink, are overweight and have dirty teeth,* The Times of Malta, Saturday, June 5th, 2004, 4.

Heath, D. (2000) *Drinking occasions: Comparative perspectives on alcohol and culture,* Philadelphia, PA: Brunner /Mazel, 145.

Henry, J.A. (1998) *The British Medical Association New Guide to Medicine and Drugs,* The British Medical Association, London: Dorling Kindersley: 441.

Hibell, B., Anderson, B., Bjarnson, T., Kokkevi, A., Morgan, M., and Narusk, A. (1997) *The 1995 ESPAD report: Alcohol and other drug use among students in 26 European countries,* Stockholm: CAN.

Hickman, T. (2003a) *Drink: A User's Guide,* London: Ebury Press, 30.

Hickman, T. (2003b) *Drink: A User's Guide,* London: Ebury Press, 158.

Hickman, T. (2003c) *Drink: A User's Guide,* London: Ebury Press, 183.

Hingson, R., Heeren, T., Zakocs, R., (2001) 'Age of drinking onset and involvement in physical fights after drinking', *Pediatrics,* 108(4): 872-877.

Home Office (2004), *Alcohol-related crime and disorder: Strategy Unit Alcohol Harm Reduction project: Interim Analytical Report,* http://www.homeoffice.gov.uk/rds/alcohol1.html, 27th April, 2004.

Home Office (2005) 'Home Office Circular 60/1995 (Registration Schemes for Doormen), in Gill, M. (eds) *Crime at work, increasing the risk for offenders, volume 2,* Leicester: Perpetuity Press Ltd.

International centre of alcohol policies (2004) *Minimum Drinking and Purchasing Age Laws,* http://www.icap.org/publications/report4.html, 18th June 2004.

Johnston, L.D., O'Malley, P. M., & Bachman, J. G. (1995) *National Survey Results on Drug Use From the Monitoring the Future Study, 1975-1994: Volume I. Secondary School Students,* Rockville, MD: National Institute on Drug Abuse.

Kellner R. and Uhlenhuth E.N. (1991) 'The rating and self-rating of anxiety', *British Journal of Psychiatric.*

Knight, B. (1997) *Simpson's Forensic Medicine* (11th edn), London: Arnold, 178.

Knop, J., Teasdale, T.W., Schulsinger, F., and Goodwin D.W. (1985) 'A prospective study of young men at high risk for alcoholism: School behaviour and achievement' *Journal of Studies on Alcohol,* 46(4): 273-278.

Legal Malta (2003) *The Maltese Law on the Maintenance of good order at places of entertainment, Chapter 40,* http://www.legal-malta.com/law/laws-of-malta.htm, 22nd April, 2004.

Lintner, B. (1991) *Living with Teenagers: Alcohol,* London: Macdonald Optima, a division of Macdonald and Co. (Publishers) Ltd, 62.

Lutzin, S. & Orem, R. (1967) 'Freedom, Responsibility & Justice: The Criminology of the New Right, in W.Amos & C.Wellford (eds), *Delinquency Prevention: Theory & Practice,* Englewood Cliffs, NJ: Prentice-Hall.

Malta Critique (1998) 'Under-age drinking gives cause for concern' in The Malta Independent, September 10, 1998, http://www.maltacritique.org/Drugs/drinking02.htm, 22nd April, 2004.

Moos, R.H., and Billings, A.G. (1982) 'Children of alcoholics during the recovery process: Alcoholic and matched control families', *Addictive Behaviors,* (7): 155-163.

Muscat R. and Rapinett, G. (2002) *ESPAD: Students survey in secondary schools, Malta, 1999, ESPAD: student survey in secondary schools, Malta, 1995,* Malta: Sedqa.

National Commission Against Drunk Driving (2005) *Preventing and Detecting Underage Drinking,* http://www.ncadd.com/preventing_pas.cfm, 18th February 2005.

National Institute on Alcohol Abuse and Alcoholism (2002), *College Drinking Hazardous to Campus Communities Task Force Calls for Research-Based Prevention Programs,* www.niaaa.nih.gov/press/2002/college.htm, 5th July, 2004.

National Institute on Alcohol Abuse and Alcoholism (2003a) *Underage Drinking: A Major Public Health Challenge,* www.niaa.nih.gov/publications/aa59.htm, 5th July, 2004.

National Institute on Alcohol Abuse and Alcoholism (2003b), *Alcohol Problems in Intimate Relationships: Identification and Intervention,* http://www.niaaa.nih.gov/publications/niaaa-guide/, 7th July, 2004.

Newcombe, R., Measham, F. and Parker, (1995) 'A survey of drinking and deviant behaviour among 14/15- year-olds in north west England' in T. Honess, L. Seymour and R. Webster (eds), *The Social Contexts of underage drinking,* London: Crown.

Otway, H.J., and von Winfeldt, D., (1982) 'Beyond Acceptable Risk: On the Social Acceptability of Technologies', *Policy Sciences,* 14: 247-56.

Primedia Company (2004) *Alcoholism / Substance Abuse, College Drinkers Pay Less, Drink More by Buddy T,* http://alcoholism.about.com/cs/college/a/aa000623a.htm, 1st October, 2004.

Public Health Service (1996) *Facts, effects, and what is alcohol?* http://uk.geocities.com/youthprojectuk/awareness/Alcohol/ALCOHOL1.htm, 15th September, 2004.

Rockerbie, R.A. (1999) *Alcohol and Drug Intoxication,* Canada: Trafford Publishing Service.

Rowell, R., (1997) *Alcohol and AIDS*, Native American HIV / AIDS Homepage.

Santrock, J.W. (1981) *Adoloscence: An Introduction,* Iowa: Win C. Brown Co. Pub.

Santrock, J.W. (1993) *Adolescence: An Introduction,* Iowa: Win C. Brown Co. Pub, 63.

Scales, P.C., and Leffert, N. (1999) *Developmental Assets: A Synthesis of the Scientific Research on Adolescent Development,* Minneapolis, MN: Search Institute.

Scarman Centre (2001a) *MSc in Security and Risk Management, Module 1,* Leicester: Scarman Centre, 1-16, 4-16.

Scarman Centre (2001b) *MSc in Security and Risk Management, Module 3,* Leicester: Scarman Centre, 6-40.

Scarman Centre (2001c) *MSc in Security and Risk Management, Module 3,* Leicester: Scarman Centre, 6-6.

Schuckit, M.A., and Chiles, J.A. (1978) 'Family history as a diagnostic aid in two samples of adolescents', *Journal of Nervous and Mental Disease,* 166(3): 165-176.

Sedqa (2004) *The agency against drug and alcohol abuse, http://www.sedqa.org.mt/,* 18th June, 2004.

Single, E. and Leino, V.E. (1998) 'The level, patterns and consequences of drinking', in International Center for Alcohol Policies 2004, *What drives underage drinking? An International Analysis,* Washington, DC.

Spear, L. (2002) 'Adolescent brain and the college drinker: Biological basis of propensity to use and misuse alcohol', *Journal of Studies on Alcohol* (Suppl. 14): 71–81.

Stress Management (2004) *Does stress cause alcoholism?* http://stress.about.com/cs/substanceabuse/a/aa092000a.htm, 25th April, 2004.

Strunin, L., and Hingson, R. (1992) 'Alcohol, drugs, and adolescent sexual behaviour', *International Journal of the Addictions,* 27(2):129-146.

Talbot L.A. (1995) *Principles and Practice of Nursing Research,* USA: Mosby Year Book Inc.

The British Psychological Society (2004) *Ethical Principles for conducting Research with Human Participants*, http://www.bps.org.uk/the-society/ethics-rules-charter-code-of-conduct/code-of-conduct/ethical-principles-for-conducting-research-with-human-participants.cfm, 9th November, 2004.

The Malta Business Weekly (2001) TSG compliments authorities and the public, http://www.business-line.com/business-weekly/archives/324/15.htm, 16th January, 2005.

The Malta Independent on Sunday, *Binge Drinking,* January 16, 2005:23.

The Social Research Association (2003) *The 2003 Ethical Guidelines,* http://www.the-sra.org.uk/ethics03.pdf, 9th November, 2004.

The Sunday Times of Malta (2004) *Alcohol abuse,* April 11, 2004, 79.

The Sunday Times of Malta (2004) *Alcohol to minors,* November 14, 2004, 6.

The Times Of Malta (2004a) *Minister wants to ban alcohol use by minors,* December 15, 2004, 18.

The Times Of Malta (2004b) *Minister wants to ban alcohol use by minors,* December 15, 2004, 1.

The World Book, Rush-Presbyterian-St.Luke's Medical Center, Medical Encyclopedia, Your Guide to Good Health (1995) 5th edition, *Alcohol abuse,* Chicago: World Book, Inc, 22.

U.S. Department of Health and Human Services (1992) *Youth and alcohol: Dangerous and deadly consequences.* Washington, DC: Department of Health and Human Services, Office of Inspector General.

University of Leicester (2005) *News: CCTV systems 'fail to cut crime'* http://www.le.ac.uk/, 03rd March, 2005.

University of Minnesota (2005) *Conceptualization and Measurement April 16, 1996,* http://www.soc.umn.edu/~xshu/lecture7.htm, 03rd January, 2005.

Virkkunen, M., and Linnoila, M. Serotonin (1997) 'In early–onset alcoholism', in M. Galanter (eds) *Recent Developments in Alcoholism, Vol 13: Alcohol and Violence,* New York: Plenum Press: 173–189.

Wechsler, H., Dowdall, G., Davenport, A. and Rimm, E.B. (1995) 'A gender-specific measure of binge drinking among college students', *American Journal of Public Health,* 982-985.

World Health Organization (1999) *Global Status Report on Alcohol,* Geneva: Author.

Young, S.E., Corley, R.P., Stallings, M.C. (2002) 'Substance use, abuse and dependence in adolescence: Prevalence, symptom profiles and correlates', *Drug and Alcohol Dependence* 68(3): 309–322.

APPENDICES

Appendix A

Copy of an introduction covering letter

University of Leicester

Department of Criminology

The Friars
154 Upper New Walk
Leicester LE1 7QA · UK
Tel: +44 (0)116 252 3946/2458
Fax: +44 (0)116 252 5788
Email: criminology@le.ac.uk
Website: www.le.ac.uk/criminology

Head of Department
Andrew Wilhs

30 November 2004

Dear

Duncan Borg Ellul – MSc Security and Risk Management

This letter serves as confirmation that Duncan Borg Ellul is studying for an MSc in Security and Risk Management at the Department of Criminology, University of Leicester. He is currently undertaking research for his dissertation on the subject of risk perception, awareness and prevention measures to reduce underage drinking and the illegal purchase of alcohol in Malta.

Yours sincerely

Tracey Dodman
Course Director

Appendix B

Approvals to conduct research in State and Non-State schools

Appendix C

A letter from the Police General Headquarters, Floriana, Malta

All communications should be addressed to the Commissioner of Police, and not to individual officers by name or appointment

COMMUNITY AND MEDIA RELATIONS UNIT
Police General Headquarters
Floriana CMR 02
MALTA.
30th November, 2004

Our Reference No.P/O Dup/P496/85/1/49
Your Reference No.

Mr. Duncan Borg Ellul,
32/1, Tigne' Sea Front,
Sliema

Mr. Borg Ellul,

Reference is being made to your request regarding crimes and alcohol.

Regarding your request for statistics regarding underage purchase, possession and consumption of alcohol, please note that it is only the sale of alcohol to persons under the age of 16 from wines and spirits shops that is prohibited by law. In this respect, this year up to the end of October, 4 persons have already been arraigned in Court for selling alcoholic drinks to persons under the age of 16.

Regarding cases of persons in possession of fake ID cards, such statistics are not available.

Finally regarding alcohol involvement in crimes please note that serious crimes, such as those mentioned by your gooself concern Magesterial inquiries and therefore these are not available.

Regards,

WPC255 Roberta Fenech
CMRU

Appendix D

Blood Alcohol Count rate (BAC)

BAC Rates

BAC RATE	Likely effects on the Normal Average Human Being
0.02% - 0.03%	No loss of co-ordination, slight euphoria and lack of shyness. Depressant effects on central nervous system not apparent
0.04% - 0.06%	Feeling of wellbeing, relaxation, lower inhibitions, sensation of warmth, flushed skin, euphoria. Some minor impairment of reasoning, memory, and judgement may also occur. This state may be referred-to as 'mild intoxication'.
0.07%-0.09%	Slight impairment of balance, speech, vision, reaction time, and hearing. Euphoria. Judgement and self-control are reduced, and reason, memory, and judgement are impaired.
0.10-0.125%	Significant impairment of motor co-ordination and loss of good judgement. Speech may be slurred; balance, vision, reaction time and hearing will be impaired. Euphoria. Such a state of intoxication is physically very evident.
0.13%-0.15%	Gross motor impairment and lack of physical control. Blurred vision and major loss of balance. Euphoria is reduced and dysphoria (i.e. anxiety, depression, and restlessness) begins to appear.
0.16% - 0.20%	Dysphoria predominates, nausea may appear. The drinker has the appearance of a 'sloppy drunk'.
0.25%	Difficulty or inability to stand or walk; total mental confusion. Dysphoria with nausea, incontinence, and vomiting. In the medical field, this stage is considered to be 'extreme intoxication'.
0.30%	Loss of consciousness, incontinence, low body temperature, poor respiration, fall in blood pressure, clammy skin.
0.40%	Onset of coma; possibility of death due to respiratory arrest.
0.40% and up	Death very possible.

(Knight, 1997:178).

Appendix E

Minimum Drinking and Purchasing Age Laws

Minimum Drinking and Purchasing Age Laws

Country	Minimum Drinking Age (MDA)	Minimum Purchasing Age (MPA)	Notes
Albania	-	No MPA	
Algeria	-	18	
Argentina	18	-	
Armenia	No MDA	No MPA	
Australia	18	18	State and Territory laws prohibit sale or serving of alcohol to those under 18 years of age.
Austria	16, 18*	16, 18	On-premise consumption is subject to provincial regulation. In general, the MDA is 16 (*in one Bundesland MDA is 16 for spirits and 15 for wine and beer). Some provinces prohibit consumption of spirits for those under 18.
Azerbaijan	-	18	
Belarus	-	18	
Belgium	16	16, 18	The MPA in bars is 18 for spirits and 16 for beer and wine. No specific restrictions apply to purchase of beer and wine in shops. The law prohibits anyone under the age of 16 (unless married or accompanied by parent or guardian) from entering a "dance hall" where fermented beverages are sold.
Bolivia	-	18	
Bosnia and Herzegovina	-	16	The MPA of 16 applies to buying alcohol for on-premise consumption (e.g. in bars). No age limit is set for buying alcohol in shops.
Brazil	18	-	
Bulgaria	18	18	
Cambodia	-	No MPA	
Cameroon	18	-	
Canada	18, 19	18, 19	The MDA and MPA are 18 in Alberta, Manitoba and Quebec, in all other provinces the MDA and MPA are set at 19. Drinking by minors under adult supervision is permitted in licensed premises in the provinces of Manitoba and New Brunswick and at home in Prince Edward Island, Alberta, British Columbia, Ontario and Saskatchewan.
Chile	18	18	
China	No MDA	18	
Colombia	18	18	
Costa Rica	-	18	
Croatia	-	18	
Czech Republic	18	18	
Denmark	16	16	Beverages with an alcohol content of 1.2% or more by volume (abv) must not be sold to persons under 16 years of age at shops where retail sale takes place. Such beverages (1.2% abv or more) cannot be brought into Denmark from other EU countries by persons under 16 years of age. This regulation does not apply

			to beer.
Ecuador	-	18	
Egypt	21	18, 21	The MPA is 18 for beer and 21 for wine and spirits.
El Salvador	-	18	
Eritrea	-	18	
Estonia	18	18	
Ethiopia	-	18	
Finland	18	18, 20	The MPA is 20 for purchasing spirits in shops and 18 for all other alcohol purchases.
France	16	16	Individuals under 16 years of age cannot enter bars, unless accompanied by parent or guardian.
Georgia	No MDA	16	
Germany	16, 18	16, 18	The MDA and MPA are 16 for beer and wine, and 18 for spirits. Beer and wine may be served to individuals under 16 only if accompanied by parent or guardian.
Greece	18	17	The MDA and MPA apply to drinking in bars. No age limit is set for buying alcohol in shops or for off-premise consumption.
Guatemala	-	18	
Guyana	-	18	
Honduras	21	18	
Hong Kong	18	18	
Hungary	-	18	
Iceland	20	20	
India	18-25	18-25	Drinking age limits are legislated by individual states.
Indonesia	-	21	
Ireland	18	18	Individuals under 18 are allowed in bars, but those under 15 must be accompanied by parent or guardian.
Israel	-	18	According to the 2004 regulations, the MPA applies to purchases from kiosks and convenience stores (previously, only applied to on-premise purchase).
Italy	16	16	
Japan	20	20	
Kazakhstan	-	18	
Kenya	18	18	
Kyrgyzstan	No MDA	No MPA	
Latvia	-	18	
Liechtenstein	17	-	
Lithuania	No MDA	18	
Macedonia	-	18	
Malaysia	No MDA	18	
Malta	**No MDA**	**16**	
Mexico	18	18	
Moldova	18	18	The MDA and MPA of 18 apply to wine and spirits. No age specifications are made for buying or consuming beer.
Mongolia	-	18	
Namibia	-	18	

	MDA	MPA	
Netherlands	-	16, 18	The MPA is 18 for spirits. The MPA is 16 for beer, wine, and distilled beverages with an alcohol percentage under 15%.
New Zealand	18	18	
Nicaragua	-	19	
Niger	-	18	
Nigeria	-	18	
Norway	18, 20	18, 20	The MDA and MPA for spirits are 20. The MDA and MPA for beer and wine are 18.
Palau	18	21	
Panama	18	18	
Papua New Guinea	18	18	The MDA for consumption in private or with meals on licensed premises is not specified. The MPA for on-licensed premises is 18 and it is not specified for off-licensed premises and supermarkets.
Paraguay	-	18	
Peru	18	18	
Philippines	18	18	
Poland	-	18	
Portugal	16	16	
Romania	18	18	
Russia	18	18	
Samoa	21	-	
Seychelles	-	18	
Singapore	18	18	
Slovak Republic	18	18	
Slovenia	18	18	
Solomon Islands	21	-	
South Africa	18	18	
South Korea	19	19	Consumption in private is at the discretion of parents or accompanying adults.
Spain	16, 18	16, 18	The MDA and MPA vary by region: some autonomous communities set the MDA and MPA at 18, others at 16. The Spanish Government is currently considering a proposal to set the national MDA and MPA at 18.
Sri Lanka	18	18	
Suriname	-	16	
Sweden	18	18, 20	Purchase for off-premise consumption: the MPA varies. Generally, for beer and cider with an alcohol content of 3.5% or less the MPA is 18, and it is 20 for all beverage alcohol with alcohol content over 3.5%. The MPA for buying any alcohol beverage in the Swedish monopoly stores is 20 years of age. Purchase for on-premise consumption: the MPA is 18.
Switzerland	18	18	Federal law prohibits supplying spirits to individuals under 18. The MDA and MPA for beer and wine are controlled by the Cantons and vary between 14 and 16.
Thailand	No MDA	18	

Turkey	-	18	
Turkmenistan	-	18	
Uganda	18	18	
Ukraine	No MDA	18	
United Kingdom	18	18, 16	The MDA and MPA are 18 in bars and off-licensed premises. The MPA for certain drinks, however, is 16 when purchased for consumption with meals in restaurants or pubs with separate eating areas. These drinks are beer, sherry, cider and, in Scotland, wine. The MDA at home is 5, given parental consent.
United States	21*	21**	* In 19 states alcohol consumption by youth under 21 is not specifically illegal. ** Exceptions to the 21 law in some states include possession for religious purposes when accompanied by a parent, spouse or legal guardian; medical reasons; in private clubs or establishments; or in the course of lawful employment by a duly licensed manufacturer.
Uruguay	-	18	
Uzbekistan	-	18	
Vanuatu	18	18	The MDA of 18 applies not only to consumption on licensed premises, but also to drinking in private and to drinking with meals.
Venezuela	-	18	
Zambia	-	18	
Zimbabwe	18	-	

(International Center For Alcohol Policies (ICAP), 2004)

Appendix F

Copies of the original and pilot study questionnaires

Alcohol drinking questionnaire

Date: _____

Dear student,

As part of my work towards an M.Sc. degree in Security and Risk Management at the Department of Criminology, University of Leicester UK, I am conducting a survey on alcohol drinking. You are invited to participate in the research study by answering all questions below.

Although the questions are quite simple to answer you may omit any question you would rather prefer not to answer or which you might find objectionable for any reason. In that case just leave it blank.

Participation in this project is voluntary. There are no right or wrong answers and/or known or anticipated risks to participation in this study. Completing and returning the questionnaire constitutes your consent to participate. Your anonymity will be safeguarded throughout the study. Responses will be completely anonymous and your name will not appear anywhere on the survey.

It is important that you answer each question truthfully and as thoughtfully as possible, if the study is to be successful. Completion of the survey is expected to take about 20 minutes of your time. When you have finished the questionnaire, please place all the sheets face down in front of your teacher.

I hope you will find the questionnaire interesting and if you have a question please raise your hand, and your teacher will come to your desk to assist.

Thank you very much for your assistance in this important project.

NOTE: THE QUESTIONNAIRE IS **ANONYMOUS**. PLEASE DO **NOT** WRITE YOUR NAME ON THE QUESTIONNAIRE FORM.

Yours sincerely,

Duncan A. Borg Ellul

Before beginning be sure to read the above. Please mark your answer to each question by making an "X" in the appropriate box.

Birth Year: ☐   **Sex:**   Female ☐   or   Male ☐

School: State ☐   or   Non-State ☐

PTO

1. Below is a list of statements dealing with your general feelings about yourself. *(Mark one box for each line to indicate if you agree or disagree)*

	Agree	Disagree	Sometimes
On the whole, I am satisfied with myself			
At times I think I am no good at all			
I feel that I have a number of good qualities			
I am able to do things as well as most other people			
I feel I do not have much to be proud of			
I certainly feel useless at times			
I feel that I'm a person of worth, at least on an equal plane with others			
I wish I could have more respect with myself			
All in all, I am inclined to feel that I am a failure			
I take a positive attitude toward myself			

2. How do you grade your performance at school? A ☐ B ☐ C ☐ D ☐ E ☐ or U ☐

3. How would you classify your relationship between you and your parents/guardians at home?

Good ☐   Very good ☐   Fairly good ☐   Poor ☐

4. During the week do you normally go out after school?   Yes ☐   No ☐

5. Till what time do you normally stay out with friends?   Until ☐ a.m. /p.m.

6. When (if ever) did you FIRST do each of the following? *(Mark one box for each line)*

	Never	10 years old or less	11 years old	12 years old	13 years old	14 years old	15 years old
Drink beer (at least one glass)							
Drink wine (at least one glass)							
Get drunk on alcohol							

7. How much beer did you drink the last time you had alcohol? *(Do not include low alcohol beer)*

I never drink beer   ☐

I did not drink beer on my last drinking occasion   ☐

Less than a regular bottle or can   ☐

1-2 regular bottles or cans   ☐

3-5 regular bottles or cans   ☐

6 or more regular bottles or cans   ☐

PTO

8. How much liquor (e.g. whisky, brandy, gin, vodka, baileys, malibu, others) did you drink the last time you had alcohol?

I never drink liquor ☐

I did not drink liquor on my last drinking occasion ☐

Less than a drink ☐

1-2 drinks ☐

3-4 drinks ☐

5 drinks or more ☐

9. The last time you had an alcoholic drink, did you drink any wine? If so, how much? *(Include also wine mixed with other beverages)*

I never drink wine ☐

I did not drink wine on my last drinking occasion ☐

Less than a glass ☐

1-2 glasses ☐

Half a bottle ☐

A bottle or more ☐

10. On how many occasions *(if any)* **have you had any alcoholic beverage to drink?** *(Mark one box for each line)*

	0	1-2	3-5	6-9	10-19	20-39	40 or more
In your lifetime							
During the last 12 months							
During the last 30 days							

11. How much do you usually drink on a night out? _____

12. In which of the following places do you usually drink? *(Mark all which apply)*

Never drink alcohol ☐   In a pub or bar ☐

At a disco or nightclub ☐   From a supermarket ☐

From another shop ☐   At home ☐

From someone selling alcohol from their

home, a vehicle, a shed/garage or on the street ☐   At school ☐

At someone else's home ☐   In a rented flat ☐

PTO

Out on the street, in a park, beach,
or other open area ☐

In a restaurant ☐   At the village feast ☐

Other (please specify) _____

13. Name few clubs in Paceville, which you think, are the most popular amongst teenagers.

_____

_____

14. How would you describe the atmosphere in Paceville?

_____

_____

15. When teens go to clubs or bars in Paceville, do bouncers *(security)* **ask for Identity cards?** Yes ☐ No ☐

16. What do you think of a person who does not drink alcohol and does not go to Paceville?

_____

_____

17. Name some places where youngsters can go and entertain themselves instead of Paceville.

_____

_____

18. How many times in the last month you have felt drunk? *(Mark one box for each line)*

☐ 0   ☐ 1-2   ☐ 3-5   ☐ 6-9   ☐ 10 or more occasions

19. Who do you usually drink with?

_____

_____

PTO

20. What is (are) the reason (s) for you to drink alcohol? *(Mark all which apply)*

I want to feel good ☐

I do not want to stand out from the group ☐

I have nothing else to do ☐

I want to forget my problems ☐

I want to be like my friends ☐

I know that it is harmful but I don't care ☐

Other reason (s), please specify:

_____

21. Do you think you will be drinking alcohol when you are twenty-five?   Yes ☐   No ☐   I don't know ☐

22. How likely it is that each of the following would happen to you personally, if you drink alcohol? *(Mark one box for each line)*

	Very likely	Likely	Unsure	Unlikely	Very unlikely
Feel relaxed					
Feel happy					
Forget my problems					
Feel more friendly and outgoing					
Have a lot of fun					
Get a hangover					
Mixing with drugs					
Feel sick					
I miss a day (or part of a day) of school					
I get into fights or causing trouble					
Getting in to trouble with the police					
I spend too much money on alcohol					
Not be able to stop drinking					
Do something I would regret					
I can't remember some of the things I did					

23. Have you ever had any of the following problems because of your alcohol use? *(Mark one box for each line)*

	Never	Once or twice	3 times or more
Quarrel or argument			
Scuffle or fight			
Accident or injury			
Loss of money or other valuable items			
Damage to objects or clothing			
Reduced your performance at school or at work			
Made you engage in unwanted sexual experience			
Made you engage in unprotected sex			
Driving a motor/car under the influence of alcohol			
Victimised by robbery or theft			
Trouble with police			

24. Has any adult, bought alcohol for you during the last three years?   Yes ☐   No ☐

25. If yes, who? (was it your parents, friends, others) *(Please specify)*.

_____

_____

_____

26. Do you have any of your relatives or friends who after drinking alcohol, acts aggressively? Yes ☐ No ☐

27. What do you know about Sedqa and Caritas?

_____

_____

_____

_____

28. Below is a list of reasons why some people do NOT drink alcohol. Read the list and tick each item to show whether you personally agree or disagree. *(Mark one box for each line)*

	Agree	Disagree
Drinking is bad for your health		
Drinking costs too much		
I have religious reasons for not drinking		
People who drink lose control in an unpleasant way		
It is hard to stop drinking once you start the habit		
My parents disapprove strongly of people who drink		
Drinking makes you put on weight		
Drinking has destroyed somebody that I know well		
Alcohol tastes horrible		
Some of the effects, e.g. hangovers, dizziness and vomiting are awful		
Drinking is more likely to lead to crime and violence		
Drinking is against my principles		
Drinking is more likely to lead to serious accidents		
Drinking is more likely to have bad effects on family life		
Some other reason. Which?		

29. Do you think that the Maltese Law prohibits youth at your age from drinking alcohol? Yes ☐ No ☐

30. If you were a member of parliament, what laws would you pass with regards to alcohol?

_____

_____

_____

_____

Thanks for your participation

PTO

Date:

Dear student,

As part of my work towards an M.Sc. degree in Security and Risk Management at the Department of Criminology, University of Leicester UK, I am conducting a survey on alcohol drinking. You are invited to participate in the research study by answering the attached, questionnaire.

Although the questions are quite simple to answer you may omit any question you would rather prefer not to answer or which you might find objectionable for any reason. In that case just leave it blank.

Participation in this project is voluntary. There are no right or wrong answers and/or known or anticipated risks to participation in this study. Completing and returning the questionnaire constitutes your consent to participate. Your anonymity will be safeguarded throughout the study. Responses will be completely anonymous and your name will not appear anywhere on the survey.

It is important that you answer each question truthfully and as thoughtfully as possible, if the study is to be successful. Completion of the survey is expected to take about 20 minutes of your time. When you have finished the questionnaire, please place all the sheets face down in front of your teacher.

I hope you will find the questionnaire interesting and if you have a question please raise your hand, and your teacher will come to your desk to assist.

Thank you very much for your assistance in this important project.

NOTE: THE QUESTIONNAIRE IS **ANONYMOUS**. PLEASE DO **NOT** WRITE YOUR NAME ON THE QUESTIONNAIRE FORM.

Yours sincerely,

Duncan A. Borg Ellul

Alcohol drinking questionnaire

Before beginning be sure to read the instructions on the cover. Please mark your answer to each question by making an "X" in the appropriate box.

School: Government _____   or   Church _____

Sex: Female _____   or   Male _____

Birth Year: 19 _____

1. Below is a list of statements dealing with your general feelings about yourself. *(Mark one box for each line to indicate if you agree or disagree)*

	Agree	Disagree
On the whole , I am satisfied with myself		
At times I think I am no good at all		
I feel that I have a number of good qualities		
I am able to do things as well as most other people		
I feel I do not have much to be proud of		
I certainly feel useless at times		
I feel that I'm a person of worth, at least on an equal plane with others		
I wish I could have more respect with myself		
All in all, I am inclined to feel that I am a failure		
I take a positive attitude toward myself		

2. How do you grade your performance at school?

A _____, B _____, C _____, D _____, E _____, or U _____

3. How would you classify your relationship between you and your parents/guardians at home?

Good_____   Very good _____   Fairly good _____   Poor _____

4. During the week do you normally go out after school?

Yes_____   No _____

5. Do you go out at weekends?

Yes_____   No _____

6. Till what time do you normally stay out with friends?

Till ____:____ hrs

7. If you spend the night out during the week/weekends, where do you normally go?
(Please name the place e.g. Paceville)

_____

_____

_____

_____

_____

8. If you go to Paceville, describe in your own words the atmosphere in this place.

_____

_____

_____

_____

_____

9. Name 3 to 5 clubs in Paceville, which you think, are the most popular amongst teenagers

_____

_____

_____

_____

_____

10. When (if ever) did you FIRST do each of the following things?
(Mark one box for each line)

Never	10 years old or less	11 years old	12 years old	13 years old	14 years old	15 years old
(a) (Drink beer (at least one glass)						
(b) Drink wine (at least one glass)						
(c) Get drunk on alcohol						

11. How much beer did you drink the last time you had alcohol?
(Do not include low alcohol beer)

I never drink beer   _____

I did not drink beer on my last drinking occasion   _____

Less than a regular bottle or can (<50cl)   _____

1-2 regular bottles or cans (50-100cl)   _____

3-4 regular bottles or cans (101-200cl)   _____

5 or more regular bottles or cans (>)   _____

4

12. How much liquor (e.g. whiskey brandy gin, vodka, baileys, malibu, others) did you drink the last time you had alcohol?

I never drink liquor	_____
I did not drink liquor on my last drinking occasion	_____
Less than a drink	_____
1-2 drinks	_____
3-5 drinks	_____
6 drinks or more	_____

13. The last time you had an alcoholic drink, did you drink any wine? If so, how much?
(include also wine mixed with other beverages)

I never drink wine	_____
I did not drink wine on my last drinking occasion	_____
Less than a glass (<10cl)	_____
1-2 glasses (10-20cl)	_____
Half a bottle (37cl)	_____
A bottle or more ($\geq$75cl)	_____

14. On how many occasions *(if any)* **have you had any alcoholic beverage to drink?**

(Mark one box for each line)

Number of occasions

	0	1-2	3-5	6-9	10-19	20-39	40 or more
(a) In your lifetime							
(b) During the last 12 months							
(c) During the last 30 days							

15. How many times in the last month you have felt very drunk or drunk? *(Mark one box for each line)*

Number of occasions

0 ____   1-2 ____   3-5 ____   6-9 ____   10 or more ____

16. In which of the following places do you usually drink?
(Mark all that apply)

- Never drink alcohol _____
- In a pub or bar _____
- At a disco or nightclub _____
- From a supermarket _____
- From another shop _____
- From someone selling alcohol from their
  home, a vehicle, a shed/garage or on the street _____
- At home _____
- At school _____
- At someone else's home _____
- Out on the street, in a park, beach,
- or other open area _____
- In a rented flat _____
- In a restaurant _____
- At the village fiestas _____
- Other (please describe) _____

17. Who do you usually drink with?

_____

_____

_____

_____

18.   What is (are) the reason (s) for you to drink alcohol
(Mark all that apply)

I want to feel good   _____

I do not want to stand out from the group   _____

I have nothing else to do   _____

I want to forget my problems   _____

I want to be like my friends   _____

I know that it is harmful but I don't care   _____

Other reason (s), please specify

_____

_____

_____

_____

19. Do you think you will be drinking alcohol when you are twenty-five?

No   _____

Yes   _____

I don't know   _____

20. How likely it is that each of the following would happen to you personally, if you drink alcohol?
(Mark one box for each line)

	Very likely	Likely	Unsure	Unlikely	Very unlikely
(a) Feel relaxed					
(b) Feel happy					
(c) Forget my problems					
(d) Feel more friendly and outgoing					
(e) Have a lot of fun					
(f) Get a hangover					
(n)Mixing with drugs					
(g) Feel sick					
(h) I miss a day (or part of a day) of school					
(i) I get into fights or causing trouble					
(j) Getting in to trouble with the police					
(k) I spend too much money on alcohol					
(l) Not be able to stop drinking					
(m) Do something I would regret					
(n)I can't remember some of the things I did					

21. Have you ever had any of the following problems because of your alcohol use?

(Mark one box for each line)

	Never	Once or twice	3 times or more
(a) Quarrel or argument			
(b) scuffle or fight			
(c) Accident or injury			
(d) Loss of money or other valuable items			
(e) Damage to objects or clothing			
(f) Reduced your performance at school or at work			
(g) Made you engage in unwanted sexual experience			
(h) Made you engage in unprotected sex			
(i) Driving a motor/car under the influence of alcohol			
(j) Victimised by robbery or theft			
(k) Trouble with police			

22. Has any adult, bought alcohol for you during the last three years?

Yes _____ No _____

23. If yes, who? (was it your parents, friends, others)
(Please specify)

_____

_____

_____

_____

24. Do you have any of your relatives (or friends???) who after drinking alcohol, acts aggressively?.

Yes _____ No _____

25. What do you know about Sedqa and Caritas?
(Please describe as fully as possible)

_____

_____

_____

_____

_____

26. When teens go to clubs or bars in Paceville, do bouncers *(security)* **ask for Identity cards?**

Yes _____ No _____

27. Name some places where youngsters can go and entertain themselves instead of Paceville

_____

_____

_____

_____

_____

28. Below is a list of reasons why some people do NOT drink alcohol. Read through the list and tick each item to show whether you personally agree or disagree. *(Mark one box for each line)*

	Agree	Disagree
(a) Drinking is bad for your health		
(b) Dinking costs too much		
(c) I have religious reasons for not drinking		
(d) People who drink lose control in an unpleasant way		
(e) It is hard to stop drinking once you start the habit		
(f) My parents disapprove strongly of people who drink		
(g) Drinking makes you put on weight		
(h) Drinking has destroyed somebody that I know well		
(i) Alcohol tastes horrible		
(j) Some of the effects, e.g. hangovers, dizziness and vomiting are awful		
(k) Drinking is more likely to lead to crime and violence		
(l) Drinking is against my principles		
(m) Drinking is more likely to lead to serious accidents		
(n) Drinking is more likely to have bad effects on family life		
(o) Some other reason. Which?		

29. Do you think that the law of Malta prohibits youth at your age drinking alcohol?

Yes _____ No _____

30. If you were a member of parliament, what laws would you pass with regards to alcohol?

_____

_____

_____

Thanks for your participation

Appendix G

Alcohol consumed during the last drinking occasion

Table A1

Alcohol consumed during the last drinking occasion.

Choices of drinks	BOYS Number of participants 99 (41%)	GIRLS Number of participants 142 (59%)
BEER		
Never drink beer	16 (16%)	65 (46%)
Did not drink beer on that occasion	21 (21%)	23 (16%)
Less than a regular bottle or can	15 (15%)	29 (20%)
1-2 regular bottles or cans	20 (20%)	18 (13%)
3-5 regular bottles or cans	15 (15%)	6 (4%)
6 or more regular bottles or cans	12 (12%)	1 (1 %)

	BOYS	GIRLS
LIQUOR		
Never drink liquor	26 (26%)	42 (30%)
Did not drink liquor on that occasion	14 (14%)	16 (11%)
Less than a drink	14 (14%)	14 (10%)
1-2 drinks	18 (18%)	29 (20%)
3-4 drinks	15 (15%)	25 (18%)
5 drinks or more	12 (12%)	16 (11%)

	BOYS	GIRLS
WINE		
Never drink wine	15 (15%)	41 (29%)
Did not drink wine on that occasion	22 (22%)	26 (18%)
Less than a glass	15 (15%)	31 (22%)
1-2 glasses	29 (29%)	22 (15%)
Half a bottle	9 (9%)	15 (11%)
A bottle or more	9 (9%)	7 (5%)

Appendix H

*The most popular drinking venues
amongst young people aged 13-15 years old*

Table A2

The most popular drinking venues amongst young people aged 13-15 years old

Drinking venues	BOYS Number of participants 99 (41%)	GIRLS Number of participants 142 (59%)
Never drink alcohol	6 (6%)	31 (22%)
At a disco or nightclub	62 (63%)	69 (49%)
From another shop	27 (27%)	8 (6%)
From someone selling alcohol from their home, vehicle or shed/garage or on the street	12 (12%)	8 (6%)
At someone else's home	27 (28%)	33 (23%)
In a rented flat	8 (8%)	11 (8%)
In a restaurant	54 (55%)	46 (32%)
In a pub or bar	50 (51%)	59 (42%)
From a super market	3 (3%)	1 (1%)
At home	48 (48%)	42 (30%)
At school	6 (6%)	2 (2%)
Out on the street, in a park, beach or other open area	27 (27%)	20 (14%)
At the village fiestas	49 (49%)	36 (25%)

Appendix I

Alcohol drinking in lifetime amongst students (13-15 years old)

Table A3

Alcohol drinking in lifetime amongst students 13-15 years old

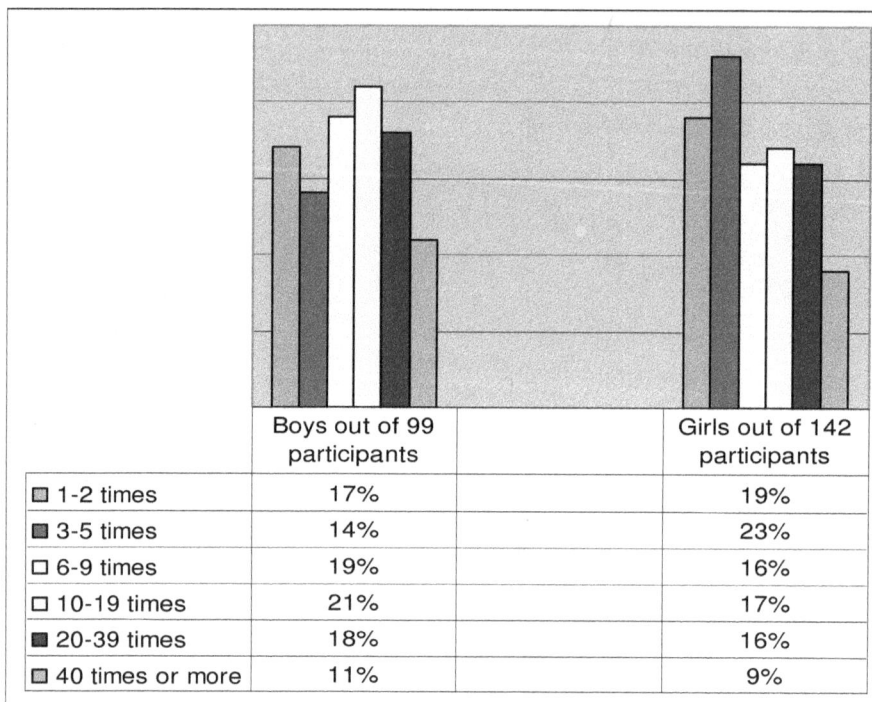

	Boys out of 99 participants		Girls out of 142 participants
▣ 1-2 times	17%		19%
▦ 3-5 times	14%		23%
☐ 6-9 times	19%		16%
☐ 10-19 times	21%		17%
■ 20-39 times	18%		16%
▣ 40 times or more	11%		9%

Appendix J

Frequency of alcohol use amongst students 13-15 years old

Table A4

Frequency of alcohol use amongst students 13-15 years old

Self grading at school	A	B	C	D	E	U
Boys' Self-Grading – State School						
13 years	7%	64%	29%	0%	0%	0%
14 years	15%	38%	27%	0%	10%	10%
15 years	0%	15%	61%	15%	6%	3%
Boys' Self-Grading – Non-State School						
13 years	0%	0%	0%	0%	0%	0%
14 years	11%	41%	29%	11%	0%	8%
15 years	10%	50%	30%	0%	0%	10%
Girls' Self-Grading – State School						
13 years	19%	25%	43%	0%	13%	0%
14 years	0%	27%	64%	9%	0%	0%
15 years	5%	44%	46%	5%	0%	0%
Girls' Self-Grading – Non-State School						
13 years	13%	74%	13%	0%	0%	0%
14 years	24%	40%	30%	3%	3%	0%
15 years	20%	50%	25%	3%	2%	0%

Appendix K

Students' relationships with Parents/Legal guardians at Home

Table A5

Students' Relationships with Parents/Legal guardians at Home

	Good	Very Good	Fairly Good	Poor
Boys' Relationships – State School				
13 years	36%	57%	7%	0%
14 years	44%	44%	6%	6%
15 years	47%	35%	15%	3%
Boys' Relationships – Non-State School				
13 years	0%	0%	0%	0%
14 years	65%	29%	6%	0%
15 years	15%	50%	20%	15%
Girls' Relationships – State School				
13 years	57%	36%	7%	0%
14 years	42%	16%	42%	0%
15 years	70%	16%	10%	4%
Girls' Relationships – Non-State School				
13 years	43%	37%	20%	0%
14 years	30%	30%	30%	10%
15 years	50%	30%	15%	5%

Appendix L

Guidelines on Alcoholic Drink Advertising

"Linji Gwida Dwar Reklamar ta' Xorb Alkoholiku"

Guidelines on Alcoholic Drink Advertising

1. Applicability of Guidelines

1.1 These Guidelines shall be read in conjunction with paragraph 19 of the Third Schedule to the Broadcasting Act (Cap. 350 of the Laws of Malta), and shall apply principally to advertisements for alcoholic drinks. However the incidental portrayal of alcoholic consumption in advertisements for other products and services shall always be carefully considered to ensure that it does not contradict the spirit of these guidelines.

2. Distribution of advertisements for alcohol

2.1 Advertisements for alcoholic drinks shall not be broadcast before 7.00 p.m.

3. Protection of young people

3.1 Alcoholic drink advertising shall not be directed at people under 18 years of age or use treatments likely to be of particular appeal to them.

3.2 Advertisements for alcoholic drinks shall not include any personality whose example people under 18 years of age are likely to follow or who has a particular appeal to people under 18 years of age.

3.3 Children shall not be seen or heard in advertisements for alcoholic drinks.

4. Unacceptable treatments

4.1 Advertisements shall not blatantly imply that drinking is essential to social success or acceptance or that refusal is a sign of weakness. Nor shall they blatantly imply that the successful outcome of a social occasion is dependent on the consumption of alcohol.

4.2 Advertisements shall not suggest

Linji Gwida Dwar Reklamar ta' Xorb Alkoholiku

1. Applikazzjoni ta' dawn il-Linji Gwida

1.1 Dawn il-Linji Gwida ghandhom jinqraw flimkien mal-paragrafu 19 tat-Tielet Skeda g]all-Att dwar ix-Xandir (Kap. 350 tal-Ligijiet ta' Malta), u ghandhom japplikaw ghar-reklamar ta' xorb alkoholiku. Il-wiri b'mod incidentali ta' konsum ta' alko]ol f'reklami ghal prodotti u servizzi ohra ghandu dejjem jigi kkunsidrat sabiex jigi zgurat li dan ma jmurx kontra l-ispirtu ta' dawn il-Linji Gwida.

2. Tqassim ta' reklamar ghal alkohol

2.1 Reklamar ghal xorb alkoholiku m'ghandux jixxandar qabel is-7.00p.m.

3. Protezzjoni taz-zghazagh

3.1 Reklamar ghal xorb alkoholiku m'ghandux ikun indirizzat lejn persuni ta' taht it-18-il sena jew juza trattamenti li jkun jappella partikolarment ghalihom.

3.2 Reklamar ghal prodotti u trattament medicinali li jirrikjedu ricetta ghall-uzu mill-bnedmin biss mhumiex permessi.

3.3 Tfal m'ghandhomx jintwerew jew jinstemghu f'reklamar ghal xorb alkoholiku.

4. Trattamenti inacettabbli

4.1 Ir-reklamar m'ghandux jimplika b'mod ovvju illi x-xorb huwa essenzjali ghas-success socjali jew ghal accettazzjoni jew li rifjut li tixrob huwa sinjal ta' djughfija. Lanqas m'ghandu jimplika b'mod ovvju li r-rizultat favorevoli ta' okazzjoni socjali jiddependi fuq il-konsum tal-alkohol.

4.2 Ir-reklamar m'ghandux jissugerixxi

that regular solitary drinking is acceptable or that drinking is a means of resolving personal problems.

4.3 Advertisements shall not imply that drinking is an essential part of daily routine or can bring about a change in mood.

4.4 Advertisements shall not suggest or imply that drinking is an essential attribute of masculinity or femininity. References to daring, toughness or bravado in association with drinking are not acceptable.

4.5 Alcoholic drinks shall not be advertised in a context of aggressive, anti-social or irresponsible behaviour.

4.6 Advertisements shall not depict or imply excessive drinking in any manner whatsoever.

4.7 Advertisements shall not offer alcohol as therapeutic, or as a stimulant, sedative, tranquilliser or source of nourishment. While advertisements may refer to refreshment after physical performance, they shall not give any impression that performance can be improved by drink.

4.8 Advertisements shall not suggest that a drink is preferable because of its higher alcohol content or intoxicating effect and shall not place undue emphasis on alcoholic strength.

5. Safety

5.1 Nothing in any advertisement may promote drinking while driving or whilst using potentially dangerous machinery.

5.2 Alcoholic drinks shall not be seen to be consumed in a working place environment.

6. Cut-price Offers, etc

6.1 Reference to "cut-price drinks", "happy hour drinks", "buy two and get one free", "money-off coupons" and

illi xorb regolari solitarju huwa accettabbli jew li x-xorb huwa mezz biex isolvi problemi personali.

4.3 Ir-reklamar m'ghandux jimplika li x-xorb huwa parti essenzjali mir-rutina ta' kuljum jew li jista' jgib bdil fil-burdata.

4.4 Ir-reklamar m'ghandux jissugerixxi jew jimplika li x-xorb huwa ingredjent essenzjali ta' maskulinita` jew ta' femminilita`. Referenzi ghal kuragg, *toughness* jew fanfarunata b'assocjazzjoni ghax-xorb mhumiex accettabbli.

4.5 Ix-xorb alkoholiku m'ghandux jigi reklamat fil-kuntest ta' kondotta agressiva, anti-socjali u irresponsabbli.

4.6 Ir-reklamar m'ghandux juri jew jimplika b'kull mod konsum eccessiv.

4.7 Ir-reklamar m'ghandux juri x-xorb bhala terapewtiku, jew bhala stimulant, sedattiv, trankwillant jew sors ta' nutrizzjoni. Filwaqt li r-reklami jistghu jirreferu ghal *refreshement* wara attivita` fizika, m'ghandhomx jaghtu l-impressjoni li l-prestazzjoni tista' tigi mtejba minhabba x-xorb.

4.8 Ir-reklami m'ghandhomx jissug-gerixxu li x-xorb huwa preferibbli minhabba l-kontenut alkoholiku gholi jew minhabba l-effett ta' sokor u m'ghandux ipoggi enfasi zejda fuq is-sahha alkoholika.

5. Sigurta`

5.1 Xejn f'reklam m'ghandu jippromwovi x-xorb waqt is-sewqan jew waqt li jkun qed jintuza makkinarju li potenzjalment ikun perikoluz.

5.2 Xorb alkoholiku m'ghandux jintwera qed jigi kunsmat f'ambjent ta' post tax-xoghol.

6. Offerti *cut-prize*, ecc

6.1 Referenzi ghal *cut-prize drinks, happy hour drinks*, ixtri tnejn u tinghata wiehed b'xejn, *money-off coupons* u

similar advertisements that encourage excessive or immoderate consumption are unacceptable. Alcoholic drink retailers may however advertise price reductions for their stock.

reklami simili li jinkoragixxu l-konsum eccessiv jew immoderat huwa inaccettabbli. Il-bejghiegha ta' xorb alkoholiku jistghu madankollu jirreklamaw tnaqqis fil-prezzijiet ghall-*istock* taghhom.

7. Humour

7.1 Advertisements may employ humour but not so as to circumvent the intention of these guidelines.

7. Umorizmu

7.1 Ir-reklamar jista' jkun umoristiku izda mhux biex jahrab mill-intenzjoni ta' dawn il-linji gwida.

8. Non-applicability of guidelines

8.1 These guidelines shall not apply to any advertisements or promotional campaigns undertaken to dissuade the public from excessive or immoderate drinking.

8. Meta ma japplikawx dawn il-Linji Gwida

8.1 Dawn il-Linji Gwida m'ghandhomx japplikaw ghal kull reklam jew kampanja promozzjonali li jsiru biex jipperswadu lill-pubbliku li jieqaf milli jixrob b'mod eccessiv jew immoderat.

9th February 2001

9 ta' Frar 2001

(Broadcasting Authority, Malta, 2001)

Appendix M

Underage Drinking at the village feasts

www.ingramcontent.com/pod-product-compliance
Lightning Source LLC
Chambersburg PA
CBHW082357270326
41935CB00013B/1660